NEBS
MANAGEMENT
DEVELOPMENT

SUPER SERIES

THIRD EDITION
Managing Resources

Controlling Physical Resources

Published for
&NEBS Management *by*

Pergamon Open Learning

Pergamon Open Learning
An imprint of Butterworth-Heinemann
Linacre House, Jordan Hill, Oxford OX2 8DP
A division of Reed Educational and Professional Publishing Ltd

 A member of the Reed Elsevier plc group

OXFORD   BOSTON   JOHANNESBURG
MELBOURNE   NEW DELHI   SINGAPORE

First published 1986
Second edition 1991
Third edition 1997

British Library Cataloguing in Publication Data
A catalogue record for this book is available from the British Library

ISBN 0 7506 3303 4

The views expressed in this work are those
of the authors and do not necessarily reflect
those of the National Examining Board for
Supervision and Management or of the publisher.

NEBS Management Project Manager: Diana Thomas
Author: Joe Johnson
Editor: Fiona Carey
Series Editor: Diana Thomas
Based on previous material by: Joe Johnson and George Runciman
Composition by Genesis Typesetting, Rochester, Kent
Printed and bound in Great Britain

Contents

Workbook introduction

1 NEBS Management Super Series 3 study links

Here are the workbook titles in each module which link with *Controlling Physical Resources*, should you wish to extend your study to other Super Series workbooks. There is a brief description of each workbook in the User Guide.

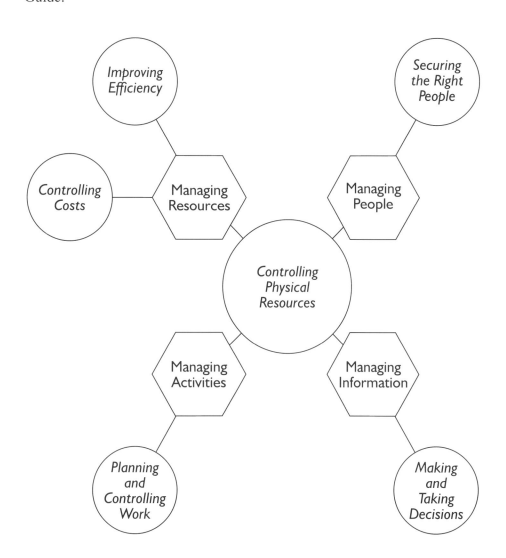

2 S/NVQ links

This workbook relates to the following element:

B1.2 Contribute to the control of resources

It is designed to help you to demonstrate the following Personal Competences:

- your ability to analyse and conceptualize, by showing that you can think clearly and objectively about the past, and to apply your thinking to present and future plans;
- your teambuilding skills;
- your ability to focus on results;
- your ability to think and take decisions.

3 Workbook objectives

All managers have resources at their disposal. It is the way these resources are used and organized that shows up the differences between a good manager and an ordinary one.

Poor managers will continually bemoan their lack of resources. 'If only I had more people (or more time, or more information, or better materials and equipment),' they will say, 'I could do a decent job'. The response to such a complaint is invariably along the lines of:

'The point is: what kind of job can you do with the resources you already have?'

This workbook is all about the management and control of resources. To control a resource, you have to monitor how well its actual performance compares with the planned performance. Managing includes determining objectives and making plans.

We will start by reviewing the types of resource and make a list of nine although, as we discuss, there are various ways of categorizing resources. We'll then consider four in more detail: people; land and buildings; equipment; and materials.

Sessions B and C focus mainly on materials, and especially the problems entailed in the acquisition and storage of these resources. Session B deals with the principles of stock control, rotating and managing stock, the receipt and issue of materials, and stock levels.

In Session C, we concentrate on the purchasing function, planning aspects of materials management, some examples of applied technology in this area, and the security of stock.

3.1 Objectives

When you have completed this workbook you will be better able to:

- contribute to the management and control of resources in your organization;
- explain the principles, and some ways of solving the problems, of stores and stock control;
- increase your skills in various aspects of materials management;
- keep your resources more secure.

4 Activity planner

The following Activities require some planning, so you may want to look at these now.

- In Activity 2 you are asked to consider the way you monitor two specific resources and to suggest improvements in this area.
- Activity 5 asks you to explain how you might give individual team members more responsibility for the control of resources.
- For Activity 30, you will need to suggest a way of improving security in your area.

Portfolio of evidence

Some or all of these Activities may provide the basis of evidence for your S/NVQ portfolio. All Portfolio Activities and the Work-based assignment are signposted with this icon.

The icon states the elements to which the Portfolio Activities and Work-based assignment relate.

The Work-based assignment involves putting forward a concrete proposal designed to reduce your organization's costs related to the management of materials.

Session A Dealing with resources

1 Introduction

'Your role, as part of the management team – and never forget that that is what you are, and certainly in the eyes of your people – is to maximize the resources at your disposal to the full limits of your authority.'

John Adair, *The Effective Supervisor*[1]

Whether it's getting people to realize their full potential, making the most of limited time, getting work done in a restricted space, or avoiding the waste of energy, the organization of resources is largely what the job of management is all about.

In this session, we will discuss the background to our subject. We begin by classifying the resources used by all organizations.

Next, we consider the steps in the process of obtaining and managing resources, and then go on to review four specific kinds of resource: people; equipment; land and buildings; and materials.

2 The organization's resources

A resource is a source of wealth. For organizations, resources are the means by which goods and services are produced.

Activity 1

3 mins

Name **three** resources that you use in the course of your work.

_____

_____

_____

[1] The Industrial Society, 1989 (page 11).

1

There are many kinds of resources, including:

- raw materials used in production processes – metals, plastics, fibres, and components of all kinds;
- machines used in making things;
- everyday materials for everyday activities, such as pens and pads;
- furniture;
- rooms, workshops and offices.

What about you – are you and your team a resource of the organization?

There are several ways to classify resources.

From the point of view of an economist, resources are classified into: land, capital, and labour.

- **Land** is the economic term used to describe all natural resources. Under this category would be included natural raw materials such as mined metals, and the ground on which work is done.
- **Capital** encompasses all non-natural resources, such as money, machinery, buildings and vehicles.
- **Labour** is a term for the human resources of an organization.

Another classification of organizational resources is: money, manpower, machines and materials – the four Ms.

However, it's useful to break down resources into rather more categories than either of these two groupings do. We will list nine different types of resource.

- Materials are components, raw materials (the inputs to a manufacturing process), consumables and other items upon which work may be done, or which aid people in doing work

  Every organization uses materials of some kind or other. Hospitals use syringes, bandages and blood. Caterers use foods and spices. Computer bureaux use floppy disks, ribbons and paper. All materials cost money, and must usually be stored somewhere, ready for use.

- Equipment is all the tools, machines, and other apparatus needed for making and measuring things, for protecting people, for handling information, for supplying power, and for many other applications

  Items of equipment range from safety helmets to desk-top computers to 600 megawatt generators. Two important points concerning equipment are that (a) it can be very expensive to buy and to run, and (b) it needs human expertise, if it is to be used well.

- People are all the employees, including managers

  You may be surprised that we call people a resource. After all, people are the thinking, caring, decision-making, co-ordinating, hard-working animals known as human beings. Is it unfair to label them a resource? Certainly, like other resources, they cost money, and their services can be bought and sold. But we have to be careful not to treat people as if they were goods or simply a means of production; humans only respond well if you regard them as individuals and handle them with respect.

- **Buildings are, essentially, anything with a roof and walls**

  Buildings – factories, offices, hospitals, barns, houses, schools, warehouses and so on – are usually the places where work is done and goods are stored. They are expensive, and take up a lot of space.

- **Land is where buildings are located, and where other work goes on**

  Land is often in short supply, and can therefore be expensive to buy.

  (Note that to avoid confusion, we have separated land from buildings. However, in law, 'land' includes not only the surface, but the buildings on it, the ground below and the air above. And as already mentioned, the economist's definition of land is 'all natural resources'.)

- **Information is the knowledge or intelligence which tells us how to carry out work activities, whom to sell to, what to make, and so on**

  The right information is often difficult to come by, especially at the time we need it. There is always plenty of useless information around, and a great deal of routine information that we need machines to help us process. It is often the best informed organizations that are the most successful.

- **Energy is the capacity to do work**

  We get energy from the sun, indirectly in the forms of oil, coal, other combustible matter, and nuclear materials, and directly as solar power. For most organizations, electricity (which is derived from one of the fuels just mentioned) is the main source of available energy. Of course, humans also need energy, which they get from food.

- **Finance is the money and credit that are the funds of an organization**

  Without finance, few other resources could be obtained. An organization's funds may come from personal investments, bank loans, government loans or grants, and other sources. Limited companies issue shares to raise finance, and, in a public limited company (plc), these shares may be offered to the public.

- **Time is the most elusive of resources**

  Time waits for nobody, is sometimes on our hands, and often flies. We may kill time, yet live to regret it, because we don't have enough of it. Not everyone would agree that time is a separate resource. 'If it is the time of humans we are concerned with,' they say, 'then it's part of the human resource.' But time, like other resources, can be managed, and used economically or wastefully.

3

So we have listed as resources:

- materials
- equipment
- people
- buildings
- land
- information
- energy
- finance
- time.

We should distinguish between resources and **assets**. Not all assets are resources, and not all resources are assets. The word assets is an accounting term meaning: 'the property, together with claims against debtors, that an organization may apply to discharge its liabilities'.

In this workbook, we don't have room to cover all these resources in any depth, so we have some choices to make.

We will set aside the last four (information, energy, money, and time) and briefly review the others (people, equipment, land and buildings, and materials) in this session.

Then, in the next two sessions, we will focus mainly on the acquisition, storage, and allocation of materials and other physical resources.

But first, a word about the management of resources generally.

3 Managing resources

The management of resources involves:

1   deciding what you want to achieve;

2   making plans to achieve it;

3   specifying the necessary resources;

4   locating and acquiring those resources;

5   preparing the resources;

6   controlling and organizing the resources to best effect.

The organization first needs to decide what it wants to achieve: what are its aims and objectives? There may be long-term and short-term objectives. A supermarket chain may have an overall objective to become bigger and more successful than all its rivals. Meanwhile, in the shorter term, it may decide to open three new branches, and so must then plan to acquire the land, buildings, equipment and people necessary for this aim.

The detail of these plans will include precise specifications of all these resources. The organization must answer questions such as:

'What resources will exactly suit our needs?'

'To what extent can we afford to compromise, and make do with less than the ideal?'

'Where can these resources be obtained?'

'How much money are we able and willing to spend on each resource?'

Once the resources are acquired, they must be prepared for use. The preparation will obviously vary according to the type and condition of the resource. Land may have to be cleared, buildings renovated, people trained and equipment set up.

Then, once ready, the resources will have to be organized and controlled, in order to get the best from them.

3.1 Monitoring resources

You may be involved in all the steps listed above, but much of your job may consist of controlling resources – the last step. A key part of controlling is in **monitoring** their use.

You have to know, to a more or less detailed level, about the **quantity**, **quality** and **cost** of the resources under your control.

Doing this job well necessitates (to give a few examples):

- keeping in close touch with what your team members are doing: how well they are coping, what problems they are encountering, and so on;
- knowing whether the equipment your team needs is available, and in good working order;
- being informed about the materials being used: whether they are in good supply, of the right quality, and are being used efficiently;
- ensuring that the available workspace is used effectively.

Portfolio
of evidence
B1.2

Activity 2

15
mins

This Activity may provide the basis of appropriate evidence for your S/NVQ portfolio. If you are intending to take this course of action, it might be better to write your answers on separate sheets of paper.

Following on from Activity 1, be more specific about the resources you have responsibility for. Summarize them under the following headings:

People (e.g. how many, and in what capacities?):

_____

_____

_____

_____

Equipment (e.g. what types, and what order of value?):

_____

_____

_____

_____

Materials (e.g. what kind, and what order of value?):

_____

_____

_____

_____

Land and buildings, if any (e.g. what size areas?):

_____

_____

_____

_____

Now think about the steps you take to monitor **two** specific resources under your control.

Specific resource 1: _____

How do you monitor the use of this resource, and at what intervals?

_____

_____

_____

If you identify a problem, what do you do about it, and whom do you notify?

_____

_____

_____

Specific resource 2: _____

How do you monitor the use of this resource, and at what intervals?

_____

_____

_____

If you identify a problem, what do you do about it, and whom do you notify?

Now suggest at least **one** way in which the monitoring of one of these resources could be improved. Be as detailed as you can in your answer.

_____

_____

_____

_____

_____

_____

_____

Now we will look at each of four resources in turn: people; equipment; land and buildings; materials.

4 People as a resource

There is sometimes some reluctance to see people as a resource. Hard-nosed senior managers may see them principally as a cost. Others may think regarding people as a resource is to see them in the same way as materials or machines. But they **are** a resource and one which is critical to success.

Activity 3

3 mins

How can an organization approach the problem of 'specifying' the people it needs?

_____

_____

_____

_____

Most organizations will first decide on the jobs it wants done, and the abilities they think are likely to be needed to do them. Generally, organizations are less likely to define personal attributes ('Must have brown hair, blue eyes, and good table manners').

To that end, a job description or specification is normally drawn up. The organization then tries to attract candidates who are likely to be capable of doing that job competently. In many ways, the process isn't far different from buying a piece of equipment. You don't usually start by naming a particular supplier; instead, you decide what you want the equipment to do, and then see which equipment on offer would provide the best value.

But, even before any thought is given to acquiring new people, the organization must analyse objectives, and break the overall task into 'person-sized' pieces. For example, before a school can work out how many teachers it should employ, and with which skills, it will need to know:

- the number of pupils it is expecting to house;
- which subjects must be taught, and at what level;
- how many periods one teacher can cover in a week;

and so on.

With people, as with any other resource, it's a question of:

What do we want to achieve? Which activities will help us get there? What resources are needed in order to carry out those activities? How can we get hold of those resources? How can we get the most from the resources once we have them?

In this brief discussion of people as a resource, we won't go into the subjects of interviewing, recruitment, training, motivation and other aspects of personnel management.

Instead, let's focus on some of the differences between people and other resources.

4.1 The under-used resource

People are probably the least well-developed resource. As John Harvey-Jones said in *All Together Now*[2]:

I invariably challenge every company I visit by asking them what proportion of the capability of their people they think they are using. I have yet to meet a single one claiming that they are using as much as a half of their people's capabilities if they were released. We talk continuously about the need to improve our productivity and, God knows, it is a dire need; yet we appear to accept with equanimity that in the world of work we are achieving less than half of our capacity.'

Activity 4

3 mins

If this observation is true, what explanation can you give for it? Why do you think organizations find it so hard to release the capabilities of people?

_____

_____

_____

_____

_____

_____

Perhaps you referred back to the comments after the last Activity.

Organizations usually get people to fit the jobs, rather than making the jobs fit the people. That being so, employees can only use certain specific skills, and may have little opportunity to shine in other areas. For example, a child care worker may be a brilliant organizer, but may get paid mainly for her social skills, rather than administrative ones. Or a secretary with a flair for

[2] Mandarin Paperbacks, 1995 (pages 9–10).

tactful negotiation may spend most of his time typing letters, because that's the job that needs to be done.

If the team leader or manager is perceptive enough to recognize under-developed or unused abilities in individual team members, the next problem is to find ways of using them. That's not often easy. There have been instances of organizations branching off in a new direction, when its management realized it had a pool of hidden talent in its midst, but these occasions are rare. You may have sometimes found yourself in the position of having to realize certain aims, and making the best use of available resources in doing so. The only options are in matching a given set of people to a given list of jobs; nothing else is on the agenda.

There are also other difficulties associated with developing people, including:

- the cost of arranging sufficient training, of the right quality;
- motivating individuals, so that they want to work hard and get better at what they do;
- ensuring that jobs are more challenging than boring, but without being too difficult or stressful;
- getting people at all levels involved with decision making, and especially with making decisions about their own jobs.

Empowerment is discussed further in the Super Series workbook *Leading Your Team.*

This last point has been the subject of a great deal of discussion in recent years. You may have come across the word 'empowerment'. Broadly speaking, this means allowing teams and team members to decide the best way of getting their work done, rather than working under close management. The advantages, when empowerment has been carefully implemented and is properly supported, are increased motivation and efficiency.

Portfolio
of evidence
B1.2

Activity 5

15
mins

This Activity may provide the basis of appropriate evidence for your S/NVQ portfolio. If you are intending to take this course of action, it might be better to write your answers on separate sheets of paper.

Describe the ways in which you give your team members opportunities to take individual responsibility for the efficient use of resources.

_____

_____

_____

_____

Now explain how you might increase these opportunities.

If you were to give team members more individual responsibility, what effects do you expect it would have on efficiency and morale?

4.2 Treating people as individuals

Another major difference between people and other resources is that employees should never be regarded as simply a means to an end. Organizations that treat their people as if they were items of equipment, to be used and set aside at management's whim, will never get the best from this precious resource.

As Peter Drucker wrote:

' . . . we habitually define the rank-and-file worker – as distinguished from the manager – as a man [sic] who does as he is directed, without responsibility or share in the decisions concerning his work or that of others. This indicates that we consider the rank-and-file worker in the same light as other material resources, and as far as his contribution to the enterprise is concerned as standing under the laws of mechanics. This is a serious misunderstanding.'[3]

These remarks are also relevant to Activity 4.

To avoid the mistake of regarding employees as objects, we have to realize that people don't come in bulk packages. Every person is unique, and has an individual contribution to make. Perhaps you think this is so obvious as not to be worth saying. If so, give truthful answers to the questions in the next Activity.

---

[3] *The Practice of Management* (1989), page 12, Butterworth-Heinemann.

Activity 6

2 mins

How does your organization treat temporary employees? If, say, you hire a clerk, a labourer, or a technician for a few days or weeks, is there any attempt to: (circle your response)

- get to know that person as an individual?   YES/NO

- treat the temporary employee with the same respect as permanent staff?   YES/NO

- give him or her as much support as other staff?   YES/NO

- regard the person as someone who needs motivation and job satisfaction?   YES/NO

Perhaps you were able to answer 'yes' to all these questions. It is not unknown, however, for temporary employees (and permanent ones) to be regarded by management and other staff as if they were subhuman – things rather than people.

It would be easy to fill this workbook with discussions on the subject of people resource management, but that is not our main aim. We must move on to other topics.

5 Equipment as a resource

Equipment is a term encompassing various kinds of clothing, tools and machinery. It is by its nature technical, being based on one or more kinds of technology. The word 'technology' has itself been defined as:

'the practical application of methods for using physical resources'.

Technology and competition

Now, even people with little technical knowledge recognize that technology is liable to become outdated very quickly. This fact poses many problems for work organizations. Because of competition, few organizations can afford to become complacent about their methods of producing goods or services, or the systems used in their internal processes. Every organization has to continually find new answers to the questions:

- How can we raise our quality?
- How can we lower our costs?
- How can we improve our methods?
- How can we do things better than we are doing now?

The drive for increased efficiency and effectiveness often leads down the path of either new technology, or improved methods for utilizing existing technology.

We'll look at some examples of the way in which technology is being introduced into materials management, later in the workbook.

Of course, highly technical and up-to-date equipment (such as robotized assembly lines; supercomputers; body scanners and other sophisticated medical machinery) is invariably extremely expensive to purchase and to run. This may place organizations in the dilemma of not being able to afford the investment until income increases, and not being able to increase income until the new machinery is installed. The pooling of resources is often one solution, and this is sometimes part of the rationale behind company mergers.

Equipment as a daily resource

Deciding what equipment to obtain, and when and how to obtain it, is one problem for managers. What about the day-to-day difficulties?

Activity 7

4 mins

What problems do you encounter regarding the use and control of equipment in your area? EITHER list **three** or **four** different problems, OR describe **one** particular problem in detail.

_____

_____

_____

_____

_____

_____

_____

_____

As we have discussed, equipment is often both expensive and complex. As such, it needs a special kind of management. If you use the wrong equipment, or use it incorrectly, the result can be a disaster; at best it will make you and your team inefficient. Typical problems include:

- people not being trained to make the best use of equipment;
- machines and other equipment breaking down or becoming worn;
- having insufficient equipment;
- using inappropriate equipment;
- abusing equipment, deliberately or otherwise;
- using equipment incorrectly.

13

To get the optimum value from equipment, it is important for the people using it to have:

■ a good understanding of what it is designed to do;
■ training in how to use it;
■ a proper system of maintenance;
■ an appropriate system of security.

6 Land and buildings as a resource

Under English law, land and premises are held either as freehold or as leasehold estate.

When an organization purchases the **freehold** of a piece of land, it becomes the outright owner. With certain exceptions, it then owns everything beneath the surface and all the airspace above. If the value of the property rises, the freeholder benefits; if it falls, the freeholder may have to sell at a loss. Because they cost such a lot, and because owners are vulnerable to fluctuations in the property market, land and buildings require very careful management.

Leasehold property is held under the terms of a lease. This grants the leaseholder a right to occupy the land for a fixed period of time, typically for 99, 200 or 999 years.

Usually, the lease will impose restrictions on the use to which the land can be put. The landlord may also specify that repairs be carried out by the occupier, and that rates and taxes be paid.

Apart from the use of land to build upon, either to use or to sell, it may be a more direct source of wealth, for a mining or agricultural company, for example.

Although you may not be responsible for your organization's land and buildings, it is quite possible that you are in control of a work area that is part of a building or land resource.

Activity 8

Try to **list** three aspects you need to consider when managing a work area. To give you a start, equipment access is one consideration.

_____

_____

_____

_____

You may have mentioned:

■ Access to equipment

Where equipment is needed to carry out a task, it should be in a position where team members can get to it without hindrance. The workspace layout should be designed so that the most frequently used equipment is in the foreground, while rarely used items are further from the work area. Again, safety needs to be borne in mind: it can sometimes be unsafe to make equipment too accessible.

■ Movement of people

For safety reasons, people need to be able to move about freely in their workplace. But they shouldn't find it necessary to make excessive or unnecessary movements, perhaps because materials and equipment are not close to hand. In addition, if individual paths cross too frequently, work processes may become slow and inefficient.

■ Orderliness and appearance

A well-managed workspace will be free of clutter and dirt, in order (a) to make the work atmosphere more agreeable, and more productive; and (b) to reduce hazards from fire and accidents.

The overall appearance of the workplace will also certainly have an effect on morale, and on the response of visitors. Polish and paint can work wonders in this regard.

■ Siting of materials

As with equipment, thought needs to be given to the placing of work materials, with the efficiency of the workteam in mind.

■ Grouping of staff

Should team members with similar types of expertise be situated together, or would 'skills mix' be more efficient? Different teams work in different ways, and each team leader has to consider which would be most effective.

7 Materials as a resource

In the remainder of this workbook, we will be discussing the storage, allocation, and acquisition of materials. Materials are sometimes subdivided into raw materials, components and consumables.

Activity 9

3 mins

Of the materials you use in your workplace (some of which you may have listed in Activity 2), jot down the name of **one** type of consumable, **one** type of component and **one** type of raw material.

_____

_____

_____

_____

_____

_____

Raw materials are basic substances that are processed in order to manufacture products. Paper is used to make books; silicon is a raw material in the manufacture of transistors; leather is a necessary material for most kinds of shoes; sheet metal is pressed and formed to make car bodies.

Components are parts, often having themselves been manufactured from raw materials, which go to make a larger assembly. One component of a door is its handle; some of the components of an electric lawn-mower are the rotating blades, the motor, the cable and the on-off switch; engines, wings and fuselage are all aircraft components.

Consumables are items that are used up in a work process, and do not necessarily form part of the final product. Examples are cleaning materials, glue, paper documents, masking tape, pens and pencils.

Of course, materials are needed in all organizations, not only manufacturing ones. Market gardeners use fertilizer and seeds; transport companies need vehicle spare parts, fuel and log books; financial advisers are likely to use lots of paper and printing ink; locksmiths have key blanks, oil and metal parts; county councils use large quantities of all kinds of materials.

The main problem usually associated with the management of materials is in getting them into the right place at the right time, while keeping costs to a minimum. This problem is the focus of our attention in the next two sessions.

Self-assessment 1

15 mins

1   One classification of resources we discussed was their division into:

- land: the economic term used to describe all natural resources;

- capital: all non-natural resources;

- labour: a term for the human resources of an organization.

How would you match our later list of nine resources against these three? Answer by ticking the appropriate boxes in the table.

	Materials	Equipment	People	Buildings	Land	Information	Energy	Finance	Time
Land									
Capital									
Labour									

2   Fill in the blanks in the following list with suitable words.

The management of resources involves:

1   _____ what you want to achieve;

2   making _____ to achieve it;

3   _____ the necessary resources;

4   locating and _____ those resources;

5   _____ the resources;

6   _____ and organizing the resources to best effect.

3 Complete the following cross-word by solving the clues. All the words in the answer were mentioned in the session.

ACROSS

2. Obtain (7 letters).
5. Employment bodies (13 letters).
7. Implements, machines, etc. (9 letters).
10. We don't have enough of it, but we sometimes kill it (4 letters).
11. Where organizations are housed (9 letters).
13. These are useful for making things with (5 letters).
17. There's plenty of this around, but often it's not of the right sort (11 letters).

DOWN

1. A most precious resource (6 letters).
3. Materials that can be used or eaten (11 letters).
4. Resources are the means by which goods and _____ are produced (8 letters).
6. Detailed description of what has to be done (13 letters).
8. The capacity for activity or work (6 letters).
9. Anything one has to do (3 letters).
12. We sometimes make these things before we start work (5 letters).
14. Land and other resources are _____ in short supply (5 letters).
15. Labour, toil, effort or drudgery (4 letters).
16. On which buildings are constructed (4 letters).

Answers to these questions can be found on page 80.

8 Summary

- From the point of view of an economist, resources are classified into: land, capital and labour.

- We listed nine types of resource: materials; equipment; people; buildings; land; information; energy; finance; time.

- The management of resources involves:
  - deciding what we want to achieve;
  - making plans to achieve it;
  - specifying the necessary resources;
  - locating and acquiring those resources;
  - preparing the resources;
  - controlling and organizing the resources to best effect.

- Organizations usually acquire employees after first writing out a job description, defining the skills and other qualities that match the jobs to be done.

- People are frequently an under-developed resource. They are certainly special, and must be treated as individuals.

- To get the optimum value from equipment, it is important for the people using it to have:
  - a good understanding of what it is designed to do;
  - training in how to use it;
  - a proper system of maintenance;
  - an appropriate system of security.

- Although first line managers don't often have to take responsibility for land and buildings, they are often in control of a work area.

- Materials can be divided into raw materials, components and consumables. The main problem usually associated with the management of materials is in getting them into the right place at the right time, while keeping costs to a minimum.

Session B Storing and allocating materials

1 Introduction

EXTENSION 1
You can find details about this book on page 78. This quotation is on page 1.

'The stores should be considered as a temporary location for materials needed for operational purposes, and should be planned, organized and operated in such a way that the period of residence of each item is as short as possible consistent with economic operation. The only reasons for carrying operating stocks is that the material is needed, and that supply cannot be exactly matched with demand.'

David Jessop and Alex Morrison, *Storage and Supply of Materials*

The storing of materials is not a subject that most people give a moment's thought to. A store does not seem to be an interesting place – it's just a location for holding things we want to use later. But for many, perhaps most, organizations, stores is a critical function: badly run, it can bring a company to its knees. The equation is simple: if you try to store too much, you will tie up money in materials unnecessarily, and clog up the stores area; if you try to store too little, the organization's work will be held up waiting for supplies.

We'll start this session with a discussion of the basic principles of stock control. Then we'll go on to the rotation and management of stock, the receipt and issuing of goods, and stock levels.

2 The basic principles of stock control

As we have discussed, all organizations need resources.

So far as materials are concerned, the problem is to get the correct goods, of the required quality, in the right place at the right time.

Obviously, planning is needed in order to achieve this. As these plans proceed, there will come a point when it can be said:

'We know exactly what we want, and when and where we want it. Now how can we get each specific item in the required place at the specified time?'

21

Usually, it is the timing that is the most difficult part, and there are typically two ways of answering this question. A very large organization may be able to pass on the problem to its suppliers by using **just-in-time** methods. As we will discuss in Session C, the concept of just-in-time means that the organization is very specific in what it demands of its supplier:

'We want you to supply these goods to a guaranteed level of quality, and to deliver them at precisely the time we can use them – not before or after.'

However, most organizations do not use components and materials at a rate that can justify such a system. Instead they must buy, and take delivery of, materials in advance of when they are needed. They have to check them to see that the goods are of acceptable quality, and then keep them in **stock** by placing them in a storage area, where they can be held in good condition until they are wanted.

It follows that:

stock is a buffer between supply and demand, or between the suppliers and the users.

2.1 The problems of holding stock

The first problem with holding stock is that it is an expense, not a source of profit. A retailer, for example, may have a large warehouse full of first-class merchandise; but it is of absolutely no use until it 'passes the till' and produces some income. Until then, it is a cost: the longer it stays in store, the bigger the cost.

Activity 10

4 mins

What kinds of costs are incurred by keeping goods and materials in store? Try to think of **two** kinds of cost, and say when and how they are incurred.

_____

_____

_____

_____

You may have noted that:

- The stock itself is not free: it has to be paid for. The money to pay for it comes from the firm's working capital, and as long as the goods are in store without being sold or used, that capital cannot be used for anything else. This is a nuisance, because that money could otherwise be doing something more useful, such as improving handling facilities or training the workforce. If the organization has had to borrow the capital that is tied up in stocks, the interest will have to be paid. If it is the firm's own money, it could have been earning interest.
- Stock needs space, and space costs money. Warehouses and stockrooms have to be designed and built; rent and rates may have to be paid. Racking, handling equipment and control systems have to be bought, installed and maintained. The more space used, the bigger the cost.
- There is also the work involved: the more stock, and the bigger the storage area, the more staff are needed to run and maintain it.
- You may also have thought of another reason why stocks are a cost and an expense: losses and deterioration. Even with the best-organized and best-designed storage facilities, there is a risk of them losing their value – usually called **shrinkage**. The longer the stock remains in store, the greater the risk of losses from these causes. The main causes of shrinkage are:

  - deterioration of quality
  - date-codes being passed
  - damage
  - pilferage
  - obsolescence.

Activity 11

3 mins

How might a part be made useless through becoming obsolete (that is, going out of date)?

Some, like the spare parts for old machines, may become useless when the machines are replaced. Others may become obsolete because there has been a change in the law, in industry standards, in a customer's specifications, or in market demands.

To sum up: for all the reasons we have discussed, organizations:

aim to keep the minimum stocks in the minimum space for the minimum time.

What can go wrong when this principle is applied? It is expensive to hold too much stock, but what is potentially even more damaging to an organization is that insufficient goods are available when they are needed. If this happens:

- work may come to a stop
- people may be laid off
- sales and customers may be lost.

So

having stocks too high is bad news; having stocks too low may be worse news.

Clearly, stock control can be a very important activity for an organization.

Now let's look at stock control with these two main constraints in mind. First, we'll think about ways of reducing the costs of holding stock. One way to do this is to make sure that the oldest stock is used first.

3 Rotating stock

It is very important to make sure that all the goods kept in the stores are in good condition, and that they don't deteriorate or become damaged in any way. It obviously helps to use the oldest stock before the newest. By the 'oldest' we mean the goods that have been in stock the longest.

The technique that demonstrates this principle is referred to as:

first in, first out (FIFO) or stock rotation.

The idea is that the first consignment of a particular item to be received in the stores should also be the first to be issued. The benefits of this approach are that:

- space is made available for newer consignments being delivered
- the average quality of the items in the store is as high as possible
- older items do not get lost or hidden by newer items.

There will of course be times when it is necessary to use newer stock before old, perhaps because there might be small differences in the newer stocks which affect how they can be used. Nevertheless, FIFO rotation is an important principle for stores management.

A more important reason for rotating stock, however, is to help reduce costs. The oldest goods carry the oldest costs (and prices), and if these are issued before newer goods with higher prices, this will:

- help control the general level of costs
- keep the value of the stocks in line with their 'book' values.

3.1 The two-bin system

The simplest method of stock rotation is the 'two-bin system'. The term 'bin' is used in stores to refer to a particular part of a shelf or a container and, in many cases, a 'bin' may actually **be** a bin. The basis of the system is described in the figure below, and there are many variations to be found.

Stage 1 Main stock placed in bin 1, reserve stock in bin 2 which is sealed. Orders/items picked from bin 1.	1 (main)	2 (reserve)
Stage 2 Bin 1 stock all withdrawn and stock now taken from bin 2, the reserve stock. At the stage of opening bin 2 a new order may be placed.	1	2
Stage 3 Goods delivered. Bin 1 refilled and sealed, so becoming reserve stock.	1	2
Stage 4 Procedure begins once more.		

It is quite common to have a reorder slip or 'bin tag', which is either attached to the reserve bin or prepared when the reorder level is reached. The tag or slip will be passed to the appropriate department to reorder the item.

A variation frequently used with stationery and printed forms is to insert a reorder slip at an appropriate point within the pack. When this level is reached, the reordering process will begin.

Activity 12

4 mins

If you can, identify an item of stock from your workplace which is controlled, or could be controlled by a two-bin system. Suggest a reason why this system is suitable for that stock.

_____

_____

_____

_____

_____

The two-bin system is primarily used for items or materials which are:

- standard
- relatively low unit value
- regularly or frequently used
- readily available from suppliers.

The major advantage of two-bin and similar systems is that cost savings are gained. For one thing, records, such as material requisition notes or job cards, are not usually required. Also, stock control labour costs are generally low.

The two-bin system is simple to operate, provided two key questions are answered correctly.

- What size should the bins be?
- What triggers the reordering process?

If the organization gets these answers wrong, it may have problems with under-stocking or over-stocking.

However, it should be remembered that the vast majority of items stocked at work are not as straightforward as those just described, because:

- they are non-standard items
- usage varies from time to time
- supply is not always easy to arrange.

4 Managing stock

A typical system for stock control is shown in the following diagram.

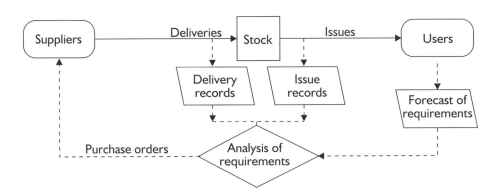

You can see that purchase orders are derived from an analysis of requirements, and that the inputs to this are:

- a forecast of what the users think they will need
- the current stock levels, based on delivery and issue records, and on physical stock checks.

Let's look a little more closely at the way in which stock levels are calculated.

4.1 The book stock formula

By knowing the stock level at a certain time (the 'opening stock'), and recording all purchases and issues, we can calculate the stock at a later time (the 'closing stock').

This formula is the **book stock formula**, and is expressed as:

opening stock + purchases – issues = closing stock

Example.   If there are 50 reams of paper in stock at the beginning of the month, 100 more are purchased on the 15th of the month and 34 are issued during the month, the closing stock at the end of the month should be:

$$50 + 100 - 34 = 116$$

Assuming the records are accurate, the actual stock level should agree with this figure. This can be physically verified, if required.

Activity 13

3 mins

Complete the following statements.

a   At the beginning of the week, 140 disk boxes were in stock. During the week, 120 were delivered by a supplier, and 160 were issued by stores. The closing balance = _____ disk boxes.

b   Opening stock + purchases – sales = _____.

c   On 1 January, 90 box files were in stock. During the month, 60 were purchased, and at the end of the month 70 were still in stock._____ files were issued.

d   Opening stock + purchases – closing stock = _____.

The answers to this Activity can be found on page 84.

4.2 ABC analysis

Because levels of stock are so critical, the stock must be closely managed. Ideally, the organization has to:

- know how much or how many of each item is in stock
- order goods in advance, to take account of the delay between placing an order and receiving the goods (called the **lead time**)
- ensure that there aren't too many of any item, because that costs money
- ensure that there aren't too few of any item, because that might impede the organization's business
- be aware of any deterioration, damage, pilferage or obsolescence, as soon as it occurs
- ensure that stock is used strictly in rotation.

Again, however, we have to make compromises, because management itself costs money. For a large stores, it simply isn't feasible to monitor every item this closely. An organization must find the right balance between the cost of controlling stock and the losses incurred as a result of not controlling it.

One way of achieving this balance is to use **ABC analysis**. At its simplest, ABC analysis is a means of categorizing items of stock on the basis of their usage value.

The usage value is calculated by:

usage value = cost of the item × number issued or sold annually

Any store, whether in a hospital, a manufacturing firm, a service company or any other type of organization, will have items ranging in usage value.

For example, a DIY store will stock items ranging from very expensive power tools, to middle-range merchandise such as tins of paint, to small packets of screws. These goods will vary in their popularity, as well as their cost and price.

ABC analysis is a modification of the Pareto principle, or the 80:20 rule as it is often known. Pareto was a nineteenth-century Italian philosopher and economist who showed that the bulk of value is likely to be held by a very small proportion of the total items. While Pareto was originally concerned with wealth, his principle was found to occur in so many other situations that the term 80:20 rule was coined. Generally, for example,

in any store, about 20 per cent of all the items held will account for about 80 per cent of the usage value.

In other words, the Pareto principle suggests that:

- 20 per cent of the stock produces 80 per cent of the value of sales or issues
- 80 per cent of the stock produces 20 per cent of the value of sales or issues.

Activity 14

Tick which of the following categories should have the greater attention and give reasons for your choice:

a   the 20 per cent of the stock which produces 80 per cent
of the value of sales or issues.   ☐

b   the 80 per cent of the stock which produces 20 per cent
of the value of sales or issues.   ☐

The question was which should have the **greater** attention. Generally, the items in category (a) would be given more consideration because the relatively small number of them produce a far greater proportion of the income. The absence of one item in this category could well have a serious effect on production or customers. However, the items in category (b) may also be important. For example, the effect of running out of invoice forms might be very inconvenient.

The conclusion must be that all items require an effective stock-control system, but that for some the system need not be so complex or costly.

In the DIY store, high-priced power tools may not sell in large quantities, but they are likely to represent a fairly high percentage of total sales. It therefore makes sense to spend more money on accounting for these items, and protecting them from would-be shoplifters, than (say) counting the number of nails in stock. This is not to say that the nails are not worth stocking; instead, it means that the loss of a few nails won't be a great financial loss.

Activity 15

To take another example, suppose an office supply company sells 4000 ink ribbons a year costing 55 pence, and sells 150 word processors each costing £650. Which has the greater usage value?

The answer is that:

$$\text{cost of ink ribbon} \times \text{annual sales} = \text{usage value}$$
$$£0.55 \times 4000 = £2200$$

$$\text{cost of word processor} \times \text{annual sales} = \text{usage value}$$
$$£650 \times 150 = £97{,}500$$

You can see that the word processor has much greater usage value, even though its annual sales are quite modest.

When the Pareto principle is applied to stock management, we usually adopt three categories, A, B and C, rather than the two categories of 80:20.

- Category A items are those small in number, but high in usage value. They are critical from the financial viewpoint.
- Category B items are medium in both number and usage value.
- Category C items are high in number, but have low usage value.

In a typical workplace, the percentage of items in each of the categories A, B, and C might be as follows:

Category	Approximate % of total items	% of usage value	Comment
A	10	75–85	High usage value, small number – critical: close control.
B	10–30	10–20	Medium number and usage value: medium to close control.
C	50–60	5–10	High number of items, low usage value: less frequent control.

Activity 16

6 mins

In your workplace, try to identify **three** stock items: one of high cost value and low quantity issues or sales; one of medium cost and quantity; one of low cost and high quantity use. Calculate their usage values.

Item 1 (high cost, low quantity)

_____

Item 2 (medium cost and quantity)

_____

Item 3 (low cost, high quantity)

_____

You may have chosen three items close in usage value, but it's more likely that the high cost, low quantity item had the highest usage value, followed by the medium cost, medium quantity item.

ABC analysis consists of the following steps.

1   Calculate the usage value for each item.

2   Rank the items in order of usage value, with the most valuable item at the top.

3   Find the total usage value of all items. Express each item's usage value as a percentage of the total usage value.

4   Calculate the cumulative percentages, working from the top.

5   Classify each item into A, B and C categories by percentage. There is no hard and fast rule for setting boundaries between categories, and this will be a management decision.

The following is a small example, showing how a list of items stocked by a furniture company worked out.

Item	Cost (£)	Annual sales (£)	Usage value (£)	Category
Wall unit	300	1,100	£330,000	A
Armchair	125	2,300	£287,500	A
Shelving unit	75	2,000	£150,000	A
Table	124	1,200	£148,800	A
Chair	45	3,000	£135,000	A
Bench	155	650	£100,750	B
Sofa	173	450	£77,850	B
Cabinet	108	560	£60,480	B
Chest	230	220	£50,600	B
Telephone table	35	400	£14,000	C
Carpet rod	2	5,000	£10,000	C
Window frame	35	200	£7,000	C
Kit of parts	15	450	£6,750	C
Wall bracket	22	250	£5,500	C
Shelf A	18	300	£5,400	C
Shelf B	17	300	£5,100	C
Hanger	1	1,200	£1,200	C
Bracket	5	200	£1,000	C
Holder	4	250	£1,000	C
Arm	2	300	£600	C

In this case, it was decided to place the items realizing around 75 per cent of the total usage value into category A, another 20 per cent or so in category B, and the rest in category C.

ABC analysis should assist in identifying the amount and nature of attention that individual items require.

Now, we'll move on to discuss two major aspects of storekeeping: receiving and issuing goods, together with the documentation associated with these activities.

5 Receiving goods

What happens when goods are received into stores?

5.1 Essential steps

Whatever industry you work in, the essential steps of receiving goods remain the same.

Activity 17

3 mins

Assume that you work in your organization's stores. Suppose a lorry arrives at the door, and you are told by the driver that he or she has brought some materials for you. What would be the first few things you would do?

_____

_____

_____

_____

_____

Before they are unloaded, you should check to see:

EXTENSION 2
British Standard BS5729 is a guide to stock control. Part 5 of this standard covers the functions and key tasks of storekeeping.

- that the goods really are for your organization, and that they have arrived at the right entrance or delivery point;
- whether the goods have some hazard associated with them: such materials should be clearly marked, and you may need to arrange for special equipment;
- what is to be done with the materials: they may be urgently required by someone, or they may be routine items to be placed into stores;
- the best way to unload the vehicle, while bearing in mind the safety of personnel, and the availability of appropriate unloading gear;
- that an area is available for the goods to be placed.

Following these preliminary checks, the goods receiving function will typically need to:

- supervise the unloading of the goods, and their transfer to the correct area;
- check quantities;
- check that the goods appear to be in satisfactory condition;
- check to see that the supplier's documentation is correct, and to record the transaction according to the organization's procedures;
- arrange for the materials to be inspected.

5.2 Documentation

Although many organizations these days have computerized stores systems, it would be useful to look first in some detail at two documents that are normally used in a manual system. This should help you to appreciate many aspects of stores documentation.

There are two possible transactions involved in the receipt of goods:

- taking in new goods, just delivered by a supplier;
- taking back old goods, which had been issued and which are now being returned for some reason.

For stores records purposes it is essential that these two transactions do not get confused. In both cases a record must be made of the transaction.

- **New** goods need to be checked against orders by stores personnel and in many organizations they will need to be notified to the people responsible for purchasing and accounting, so that they can be paid for. A **goods received note (GRN)** is usually completed.
- **Returns** have already been booked into the stores, paid for and booked out again; however, they still have to be recorded. A **goods returned note** (or debit note) is the document used in this case.

The information which appears on these documents must be sufficient for everybody concerned to understand the full details of transaction.

Although each company will have its own particular design for its goods received notes and goods returned notes, there are a number of pieces of information that must always be shown.

The goods received note (GRN)

These obviously vary from one organization to another but all contain basically the same information.

Activity 18

3 mins

Jot down **four** pieces of information you think it is important should appear on a goods received note so that each department can get the information it needs.

_____

_____

_____

_____

The words 'Goods Received Note' should appear in a prominent position, accompanied by the following:

■ **a serial number**

This identifies each goods received note (GRN), and distinguishes it from every other GRN.

■ **the date of the receipt**

Making sure the correct date is on every document helps when tracing materials; sometimes, the time of the receipt is also noted.

■ **for each item received:**

  ■ **the quantity should be recorded**

   If a delivery is made up of more than one item, each part of the delivery must be checked separately. Shortages and surpluses must be noted.

  ■ **the description should be given**

   The description helps to identify the goods; even when a code is used, a description is used to act as a confirmation.

  ■ **a code number or reference number**

   In many workplaces, codes are used, to avoid confusion caused by vague or incomplete descriptions. In a code such as 'TRP05/KP/FS': 'TRP05' might refer to the product ('typist's office chair type 5'); 'KP' to the supplier ('Kent Plastics'), and 'FS' may indicate that the goods are to be stored in the 'furniture and stationery stores'.

■ **the order number relating to the delivery**

Sometimes an order is delivered in several batches, perhaps over a number of days or even weeks. The order number is used to match each goods received note with the original order.

■ **the name of the supplier**

In case of queries, damaged goods, and so on, the supplier will need to be contacted.

■ **the signature of the person who checks the delivery**

Normally, only authorized people should be allowed to check in goods.

In addition, there may also be spaces for other items such as:

■ the method of delivery (e.g. rail, van, post);
■ the name of the organization delivering the goods;
■ the exact time of the delivery;
■ the condition of goods when received.

Here is an example of a goods received note which you might like to compare with whatever is used in your workplace.

Toys For You Ltd. Tiny Works			GOODS RECEIVED NOTE
Supplier	Date		Serial No.
	Carrier		Order No.
Quantity	Description		Reference No.
For office use		Counted and checked by:	
Ledger No.	Bin No.		

Activity 19

Which people or departments in an organization are likely to need a copy of a goods received note?

_____

_____

_____

_____

The way things are done in your own organization will depend on its size and the way it is run. In a typical large organization:

■ one copy is kept by the stores;
■ one copy is sent to the purchasing department, so they know that the supplier has delivered the goods ordered;
■ one copy is sent to the accounts department, so that payment can be arranged.

Sometimes a copy will be given to the department wanting the goods, to let them know they have arrived.

The goods returned note

All internal departments sending goods back to the stores would need to complete a goods returned note which stores can match up to the original documentation.

If the goods are being returned from outside the organization then stores will need to complete a goods returned note which can be matched up to the original sales order and to any other documentation relating to the return. This might include, for instance, a note from the salesman authorizing the return.

Activity 20

Suggest **two** items of information that should appear on a goods returned note, which do not appear on a goods received note.

_____

_____

As well as a serial number, description of the items returned, and how many were received, there would normally be:

- the reason for the return
- the department or customer returning the goods
- the job number (or other reference) for which the goods were originally issued
- the signature of the manager of the department that returned the goods.

Here is an example of a typical goods returned note.

Toys For You Ltd. Tiny Works		GOODS RETURNED TO STORE No.	
From Department	Date returned	GRN Reference	
	Date of issue		
Job No.	Supplier	Order No.	
Quantity	Description	Reference No.	
Reason for return		Authorizing signature	
For office use		Counted and checked by:	
Ledger No.	Bin No.		

Copies of the goods returned note may be required by:

- the stores, for readjusting the record of what is in stock;
- the person or department who returned the goods;
- the costing department, so that any cross-department charges may be made;
- the appropriate department who produced the goods originally.

Copies are often colour-coded, to help ensure that each department gets the correct copy.

5.3 Computerized receipt of goods

These days, it is usual for goods received notes, goods returned notes and other documents to be generated by a computerized system, and automatically distributed to the various departments, perhaps via electronic mail.

If a stores system is computerized, the following actions typically take place on receipt of goods into stores.

1   At the point where the goods are received, an operator keys in data giving details of the items.

2   The computer will check to see that this information is valid and appropriate, and, so far as it is possible to tell, that the operator has not made any mistakes.

3   If special actions are necessary, such as inspection or certification, the computer will advise the operator of this fact. It may also pass on this information to others who need to know, by sending messages to their computer terminals.

4   The computer stock records for each item will be adjusted automatically.

5   A goods received note will be generated by the computer, and copies printed out in the areas where they are required. This may not take the form that we have looked at, but may instead be printed or displayed as a summary report of all items received during a certain period.

6 Issuing goods

If you are responsible for a stores function, you will appreciate the importance of providing a first-class service in the issue of materials. This is the most visible aspect of stores work, and it is often the activity by which others in the organization will judge you.

Again, it is helpful to look at the documentation procedures.

As with receiving deliveries, two types of transaction may be involved in the issuing of goods:

■   providing a person, customer or department with the goods they request from stores;
■   returning goods to a supplier, because they are faulty, damaged or unsuitable.

Typically, the corresponding documents are:

■   a **customer order**, or internal **materials requisition**;
■   a **credit note** and **returns note**.

6.1 Materials requisition

Once again, these materials vary in detail between organizations but the key information remains the same.

Activity 21

3 mins

Jot down **five** items of information that you think should appear on a materials requisition form.

_____

_____

_____

_____

_____

One version of a materials requisition form is shown below:

Toys For You Ltd. Tiny Works		MATERIALS REQUISITION	
	Serial No.		
From Department	Date requested		Date required
Required for job:	Supplier (if known)		
Quantity	Description		Code
For office use		Authorizing signature	

Key items are the:

- serial number – to identify each individual requisition;
- date;
- quantity of each item;
- description of each item;
- code or reference number;

40

- job or batch number for which the goods are required;
- name of the department making the requisition;
- signature of the supervisor or manager of the department making the requisition.

As with goods received documents, three copies are typically required: the person or department making the requisition needs a copy; as does the stores; and the department whose job it is to cost work also needs a copy.

6.2 Goods returned to supplier

For goods returned to the supplier, we have another document, also sometimes called a 'goods returned note'. This can be confusing, as we can't tell from the name whether the goods are being returned to stores, or to the supplier. We'll call it a **returns to supplier note**.

Activity 22

3 mins

Now list **five** items of information that you would include on a returns to supplier note.

_____

_____

_____

_____

_____

A returns to supplier note should match up with the original order, GRN, and materials requisition. It would usually include:

- a serial number unique to that particular document;
- date of the return;
- quantity of each item returned;
- description of the items returned;
- code or reference number for each type of item returned;
- reason for the return;
- date of the original delivery;
- name of supplier;
- serial number of the goods received note;
- original order number;
- signature of the person authorizing the return.

You might also have included the method of return (post, rail, road transport, etc.) and the name of the company carrying the returned goods.

41

6.3 Computerized issue of goods

Where the stores system is computerized, terminals will typically be installed in a number of areas. A department requiring goods can input the relevant details, either by keying them in, or by scanning previously prepared documents.

The requisition is then printed or displayed at a terminal in the stores area. The computer will advise the stores personnel of the correct locations, and, if appropriate, a 'picking route'. **Picking** is the name given to the process of extracting goods from their locations in stores, in order to satisfy a particular materials requisition.

7 Stock levels

As mentioned earlier, it is a basic rule of stock control that we should keep the minimum amount of stocks that are necessary for uninterrupted operation. This saves money, space and work, and reduces shrinkage.

The **minimum stock** is the lowest possible level you should hold to avoid any danger of running out.

It is not the same as the reorder level: it is lower. Sometimes, a **safety stock** level is set slightly below the minimum stock level. The organization will aim to reorder so that the stock issued during the lead time, while awaiting delivery, does not eat into the safety stock.

Activity 23

Here is a diagram of a theoretical stock level record, as it is affected by issues and lead times.

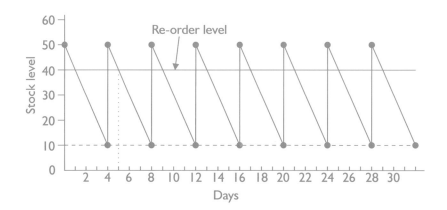

According to this diagram:

- What is the lead time for deliveries? _____
- What is the order quantity? _____
- What is the minimum stock level? _____

This is a very regular pattern – rather unrealistic, in reality – in which the reorder point is a stock level of 40, the lead time for delivery is three days, the order quantity is 40, and the minimum stock level (and in practice, the safety stock) is 10.

In the real world, the rate of use of the stock would vary, so that stock levels would sometimes rise above 40, and the reorder quantity might have to be changed on occasions. Sometimes it would be necessary to use part of the minimum stock. The point of having a safety or minimum stock is not that it should never be used: it is there for use in an emergency. A more realistic diagram is shown below:

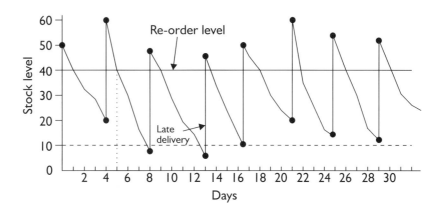

Here, levels are recorded daily, and the delivery period of three days is assumed to start exactly at the time the level reaches 40. You can see that one delivery was late, taking four days instead of three.

Self-assessment 2

1   There are seven words, plus three word pairs hidden in the puzzle below. Spend no more than five minutes in seeing how many you can find. Words can run in any direction:

The word pairs are: ABC ANALYSIS;   LEAD TIME;   STOCK CONTROL. You'll have to discover for yourself what the other seven words are. All the words appeared in Session B. Circle the words and word pairs as you spot them.

```
                        S
                    T   T   C
                    J   A   E
                A   C   R   L   Y
                E   V   I   E   C   E   R
S   T   O   C   K   C   O   N   T   R   O   L   Y   Y   R
    S   I   S   Y   L   A   N   A   C   B   A   X   S
        P   I   L   F   E   R   A   G   E   T   E
        N   O   I   T   A   T   O   R   R
        F   G   O   O   D   S   O
        B   R   X   I   D   T   R
    U   D   W   Z       S   R   I   J
    E   D   D           S   Y   M
R   R   N                   U   R   E
H   S                       E   G
```

2   Explain what is meant by the statement: 'Stock is a buffer between supply and demand.'

_____

_____

_____

_____

_____

3 The following diagram was used to explain the two-bin system, but the words have been removed. Write an explanation in your own words in the boxes on the left.

Stage 1	1 (main)	2 (reserve)
Stage 2	1	2
Stage 3	1	2
Stage 4		

4 Work out the usage value of the following items:

Item	Unit cost (£)	Annual sales (£)	Usage value(£)
Vacuum cleaner	230	500	
Microwave oven	340	750	
Refrigerator	175	330	
Installing kit	25	1000	
Spares kit	45	120	

5 Summarize the principles behind ABC analysis, in your own words.

_____

_____

_____

_____

_____

_____

45

6 Fill in the blanks in the following sentences with suitable words, chosen from the list underneath.

a Stock is a _____ between supply and _____, or between the suppliers and the users.

b Organizations generally aim to keep the _____ stocks in the minimum _____ for the minimum time.

c Having stocks too _____ is bad news; having stocks too _____ may be worse news.

d Opening stock + _____ – issues = closing stock.

e In any store, about _____ of all the items held will account for about _____ of the usage value.

20 PER CENT	80 PER CENT	BUFFER
DEMAND	HIGH	LOW
MINIMUM	PURCHASES	SPACE

Answers to these questions can be found on page 80.

8 Summary

- Stock is a buffer between supply and demand, or between the suppliers and the users.

- There are many costs entailed in holding stocks, and the general aim is to keep the minimum stocks in the minimum space for the minimum time. However, it can be more costly, and more detrimental to the organization's objectives, if stocks are too low.

- To help reduce shrinkage, stock rotation is used. One simple example is the two-bin system.

- The book stock formula is expressed as:

  opening stock + purchases – issues = closing stock

- ABC analysis is a method of determining the relative amount of attention that should be given to goods in stock. A usage value is calculated for each item, which is the purchase price times the number issued or sold; the highest usage value items then receive the greatest amount of attention.

- Typical items of documentation for receiving goods are the goods received note (GRN), and the goods returned note. For issuing of stocks, the corresponding documents are the customer order or materials requisition, and the returns to supplier note.

- Where materials management is computerized, the above documents may be issued in the form of a summary report, and automatically routed to the sections that need them.

- The minimum stock is the lowest possible level you should hold to avoid any danger of running out.

Session C Purchasing, planning, technology, and security

1 Introduction

This last session deals with four aspects of materials resource management:

- the purchasing function

  The job of purchasing is to obtain the right materials and other items, of the right specification and quality, from the right source, in the right quantity, at the right time and place, and at the right price.

  As such, it is a key function in the organization's management of resources.

- materials planning

  We look at two powerful techniques here: just-in-time, and materials requirements planning (MRP).

- the use of technology in materials management

  The introduction of technology into materials management continues at a fast pace. As we can't possibly consider all aspects of this subject, we discuss some examples of technology in the areas of inter-company communication, product identification, data storage and materials handling.

- security

  One of the main concerns of resource managers is the security of expensive materials and equipment. Our brief review of this subject is intended to help you apply the principles of good security.

Although these four topics may seem to be unrelated, our discussions of them should help us to tie together some of the themes covered earlier in this workbook.

47

2 The purchasing function

Let's just remind ourselves of the diagram for stock control, and how the purchasing function fits into the general scheme of things.

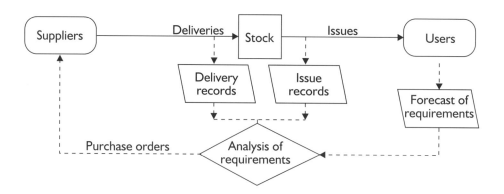

Purchase orders are sent to suppliers as a result of an analysis of requirements. This may happen when:

- new goods are needed by the users;
- the re-order level for existing goods is reached.

The existing level may be determined by visually inspecting the stock, but is more often calculated from the records of deliveries and issues.

2.1 The purchasing function

Not every organization has a person or department specifically to deal with purchases and to handle suppliers, but it's worth summarizing the activities involved in the purchasing function.

The job involves:

- finding suitable suppliers

When a new item is needed, a reliable supplier must be found. Staff who are regularly involved in purchasing will have regular contact with suppliers' representatives, and will usually be able to locate two or three potential vendors fairly quickly.

- minimizing the cost of purchases

Invariably, there will be differences in prices between suppliers, for any particular item. It is therefore important that the user or designer provides the purchasing officer with a specification of the goods, including perhaps dimensions, finish, colour, type and so on. Comparisons between suppliers' offerings can then be made on the basis of 'Which product will meet our requirements at minimum overall cost?' Quantity will obviously affect cost, as most suppliers will be willing to give discounts for bulk purchases. The purchasing function has the task of obtaining goods and services on the most favourable terms. Competitive tenders may be invited from contractors for larger value goods.

■ **arranging for goods to be delivered when and where they are needed**

Just as important as cost is delivery to 'the right time and the right place'. It is a fact of life that suppliers will sometimes give false information in order to obtain a contract. Experienced purchasing personnel will be wary of promises of delivery dates by unknown or unreliable suppliers.

■ **maintaining good relations with suppliers and with other parts of the organization**

Purchasing acts as a link between suppliers and users. Its main task is to provide a service for the rest of the organization, not only in obtaining the required goods, but in giving appropriate advice and information.

Where large quantities are being bought, and the buying organization is spending large sums of money, the supplier–purchaser relationship has to be managed carefully. It is obviously in the interests of both parties to find ways around any problems that may arise, and the purchasing officer plays a crucial role in these negotiations.

Activity 24

3 mins

From the above, what would you say were the benefits to the organization of a well-managed purchasing function? Try to list at least **three** benefits.

_____

_____

_____

_____

_____

_____

If the purchasing function is well handled, the organization should benefit from:

■ cost savings, through obtaining goods at lower prices;
■ assured supplies;
■ lower inventory costs, as a result of having materials at the place and time they're needed;
■ good supplier relationships;
■ reduced lead times;
■ reduced materials obsolescence;
■ improved quality control.

49

3 Materials planning

For any sizeable organization, the problems of stock control and planning are considerable.

As we have seen, stock is a buffer between supply and demand; it may also be a considerable drain on the organization's finances.

One approach is to do without stocks altogether.

3.1 Less than the minimum: 'just-in-time'

A very large organization has considerable power over its suppliers, who can seldom afford to lose its custom. Knowing this, the organization with the huge buying power may, in effect, say to its suppliers:

'Sorry, we're no longer prepared to go to the trouble and expense of storing your products. From now on that's your problem.'

■ Supermarket retailers try not to hold stocks except on the sales floor; if they have a stockroom, it is purely a transit point where goods-in are received and checked before being put out on to the shelves.

Retailers will always say 'if the customers can't see it, it isn't selling', so it makes complete commercial sense to avoid holding stocks in a back room somewhere. The rule for retail stock ordering is 'little and often'.

■ Large manufacturing and assembly firms also try to do without having large stocks of components. They arrange for parts and materials to be delivered at exactly the time when they are needed, to be fed directly into the assembly lines.

These are called **just-in-time** (JIT) systems. The whole operation has to be highly organized to keep these large-scale enterprises fully stocked and running smoothly at all times.

Activity 25

Write down **two** ways in which the JIT system differs from the traditional kind of stores supply operation.

_____

_____

_____

_____

Perhaps the points you identified are among the following. Just-in-time systems depend on:

- frequent and relatively small deliveries;
- very short lead times;
- close communication between the user and the supplier.

It may also have occurred to you that supermarkets that use just-in-time will also need:

- frequent, perhaps continuous, stock checks;
- computers to record the movement of goods in and out and to calculate the orders required;
- high-speed communication systems to transmit orders instantly to the suppliers.

Manufacturers that use just-in-time may depend on being able to:

- plan and forecast production rates;
- agree requirements in advance with their suppliers.

When the suppliers themselves need time to manufacture or assemble their products, advance planning is essential. The supplier and the user also need to communicate frequently in order to adjust and confirm the precise timing and volume of deliveries.

This is not possible without the aid of sophisticated technology, as the following real-life case history shows.

- A major car company, in its factory in the North East, has installed a system whereby a special coding tag on a car being built triggers a message to a supplier of carpets, boot linings and parcel shelves. There are 120 possible variations for these components, depending on colour, engine size, extras and whether the model is left- or right-hand drive. The component supplier has a factory just two miles away, and it makes deliveries up to 60 times a day.

When the message is received by computer link, machines and operators at the supplier select, trim and fit plastic extras, before stacking them in sequence and loading them on trucks in small batches. On arrival, the driver takes the stock straight to the assembly line.

The car manufacturer's management say that the system brings 100 per cent savings on inventory, 100 per cent savings on internal handling, and 90 per cent to 95 per cent savings on space, as well as productivity advantages. The dangers inherent in the system are also recognized. As the supplier's managing director says, 'If we failed to supply a part immediately it would shut down the plant.'

Activity 26

3 mins

On the whole, just-in-time has been used only by large-scale businesses. Try to suggest **two** reasons why this is so.

_____

_____

Just-in-time is very inconvenient for suppliers, who are used to a world in which most of their customers (perhaps including your organization) are content to go along with the traditional way of doing things. This includes:

- delivery during normal hours;
- longish lead times;
- grouped deliveries, perhaps covering several customers in an area;
- largish order quantities, because of the long lead times;
- buying and storing substantial stocks well in advance of when they are actually needed.

Large-scale just-in-time users have the power to insist on suppliers doing what suits **them**:

- delivery at any time of night or day;
- frequent deliveries with very short lead times;
- direct deliveries to them alone;
- relatively small orders at a time.

In practice, vendors need to be located very close, geographically, to the organization they are supplying to.

However, it isn't only large manufacturing corporations that can benefit from the concepts behind JIT. In the past few years, some small and medium-sized hospitals have adopted a policy of having 'stockless inventory systems'. This involves moving some of the supply problems to the suppliers, and eliminating stock from the central storeroom. This brings benefits of reduced costs, but obviously needs careful management and reliable suppliers.

3.2 Materials requirements planning

In manufacturing companies, and in some service organizations, the concept of materials requirements planning (MRP) can provide a framework by which scheduling and inventory decisions are made.

MRP is:

- mainly concerned with the scheduling of activities, and the management of stock;
- most useful where components and subassemblies are produced, for incorporation in the final product or service.

Examples of organizations that might benefit from applying MRP are:

- a computer manufacturing company that assembles PC boards and buys in cabinets, which are brought together in the final product;
- a hotel, which provides not only accommodation but food, a bar service, dry cleaning and so on, in the packages it provides its guests.

In both these cases, the final product to the customer is **dependent** on the provision of lower-level goods or services.

If the number of customers is known or can be estimated, then the organization knows how many of each component must be manufactured, prepared or obtained. So one of the main inputs to the MRP process is a forecast demand. Its outputs are a detailed schedule of all the items that will be required, in order to make up the final product.

> **EXTENSION 4**
> If you would like to learn more about MRP, the book listed in this extension is a useful source of information.

The other inputs are the **bill of requirements** (or bill of materials), listing all the elements that go to make a product or service; **a schedule of capacity**, showing the capacity the organization has to make things; and a list of current stock.

The essential MRP structure is shown in the next figure.

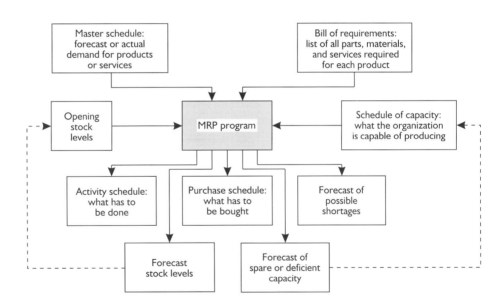

The centre box in this diagram is labelled the 'MRP program' because the calculations are done by software program on a computer. As with all computer programs, the accuracy of what you get out depends entirely on the accuracy of what you put in.

The program is run repeatedly, as new input data arrives.

Provided all the input data is correct, MRP is a very efficient method of scheduling and planning materials management. Prior to its use, materials and work scheduling was based on historical statistics, which was much less reliable.

3.3 MRPII

MRPII is based on the concepts of MRP, but in fact does not stand for materials requirements planning mark II, but **manufacturing resources planning mark II**.

MRPII goes much further than MRP, in that it is a method for planning **all** manufacturing resources. Its starting point is the organization's business plans, and its outputs are detailed instructions for:

- the purchase department
- suppliers
- stores
- the production staff.

In addition, MRPII provides detailed financial plans.

While MRPII is typically used in a manufacturing environment where products are produced in batches, it has also been applied to continuous process manufacturing, such as the production of medicinal drugs. Its implementation has achieved considerable cost savings, and improvements in production efficiency.

4 The use of technology in materials management

We have already discussed some applications of technology in materials management. Computers, in particular, have transformed the way that managers control their resources. As this technology gets cheaper, its use is becoming more widespread, and there must be few organizations now without some form of computer.

In this section, we'll look at a few more ways in which technology is making life easier (though more technically challenging!) for the people whose job it is to manage materials.

4.1 Electronic data interchange (EDI)

EDI is a method of sending documents over electronic links between one computer and another, and is commonly known as 'paperless trading'. The electronic links can be direct cable links between a buyer's computer and a supplier's computer, but more often use is made of communications networks. As a result of the use of EDI systems, buyers and suppliers are able to exchange a range of business documents including orders, goods received messages, and invoices.

As an example, assume that an invoice is to be sent from a supplier's sales ledger system to its customer's accounts payable system. Using EDI, the steps involved at the supplier's end are to:

■ **extract** the invoice-related data from the sales ledger database;
■ **format** this data into a standard form suitable for electronic transmission;
■ **transmit** the data to the trading partner, by establishing a communication route, and sending the data along the transmission line.

At the customer end, the corresponding steps are to:

■ **receive** the data via the communication link, and recognize it for what it is;
■ **reformat** the data into a form suitable for the accounts payable system;
■ **update** the accounts payable system.

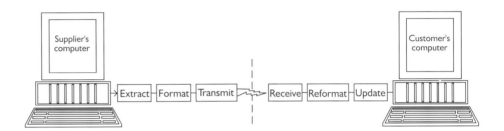

There are many benefits to be gained from closer contact and liaison between buyer and supplier, but one notable effect on stock control procedures may be a reduction in lead-times because of the faster direct contact. When compared with traditional transmission methods, EDI offers considerable cost savings.

4.2 Bar coding

You will no doubt be familiar with the bar code system used to identify and price many types of goods sold in supermarkets and other retail outlets. These consist of a series of dark bars, separated by spaces, as shown in this example:

The bars are read by a device that sends a beam of light onto the bar code panel, and detects their reflections, or by a 'light pen' which must be passed across the bar code.

Bar coding is also employed in many industrial applications, for item identification. There are several types of coding in use.

The main benefits that may be gained from using a bar code system include:

■ the speed of recording information,
■ and the level of detail which may be encoded.

4.3 CD ROMs

Another problem of stores management for large organizations is the difficulty of storing vast amounts of data, while still making the information available to users. One answer is the CD ROM (compact disk read only memory).

CD ROMs are now familiar objects in many homes, where they are used for holding audio data (e.g. music) and computer information (e.g. electronic encyclopaedias).

Once the data has been stored on the disk, it can be read by any user who has the necessary CD drive attached to a computer. Software enables the data to be searched via keywords, and the information is much easier to work with than paper printouts.

4.4 The use of robots in materials handling

Robots have been employed in industry for a number of years. By 'robot', we mean a machine capable of carrying out a complex series of actions automatically. Robots are especially useful where repetitive but precise movements need to be made.

One example of a robot is the **automated guided vehicle (AGV).** This is typically employed in moving heavy or palleted goods around a warehouse. There are a number of guidance systems for AGVs. They may follow the path of:

■ wires laid beneath the floor – these wires create a magnetic field that is detected by the steering system of the AGV;
■ painted white lines on the floor, the AGV detecting the position of these using light sensors;
■ infra-red or visible beams, which are again detected with appropriate sensors.

Alternatively, the AGV may be free-ranging, and kept under control via a computer that sends radio signals.

56

Activity 27

3 mins

Suggest **two** or more advantages of using robots such as AGVs in materials handling.

_____

_____

_____

_____

_____

_____

Robots such as AGVs hold several advantages where the initial expense can be justified.

- Robots are able to work for longer periods of time than can people, without becoming tired or bored.
- Work is generally done more consistently, and faster, than by humans.
- Their ability to operate with precision usually results in fewer incidents of damage.
- Robots often improve an organization's health and safety record, as there are fewer humans doing awkward jobs or lifting heavy weights.

Now we move to quite a different aspect of materials management: security.

5 Security

Good security measures will protect interests, property and even lives. It is not pessimistic to set up a security system, but realistic. To believe that all employees are honest is to be naive. It's an interesting and revealing fact that the most common security problems found in the world of industry and commerce are:

- theft, in general;
- theft by employees of the property and information of the organization;
- fraud, again by employees.

5.1 The conditions for theft

There are four conditions that must be present if an act of theft or pilfering is to occur. There must be:

| Something to steal | A thief to do the stealing | The opportunity to steal | A means of removing the goods |

If any one of these conditions is removed, the theft will either not take place, or will not be successful.

The more desirable something appears to be, the greater the temptation to steal it.

Assuming there is something valuable that a thief would consider worth stealing, it isn't sensible to advertise the fact. There is an expression in the security industry which sums up two important principles; it is:

the *need to know*
and
the *need to go*

This reminds us that:

- information that might be useful to lawbreakers should be restricted to those with a **need to know**;
- to maintain good security, it is best to restrict people to those areas where they **need to go**.

Thieves may break in from outside, or they may be employees or visitors already on the premises. To reduce the number of potential thieves who might target your premises, you should:

It is a mistake to 'hush up' breaches of security, perhaps through fear of bad publicity. When police officers arrive on the premises, thieves get very worried.

- be very careful about the kind of people you recruit (including temporary and part-time staff)

Many organizations take a great deal of trouble to 'screen' or vet prospective employees, by taking up references from previous employers, and so on. This is done to try to make sure that the new recruits have a previous record of being honest.

- work closely with the local police on matters of security.

However, the most rewarding approaches to reducing theft are to minimize the opportunity to steal, and to make it difficult for thieves to remove the goods.

Reducing the opportunity

One way to reduce the opportunity to steal is to control access to areas where there are valuable goods.

Activity 28

3 mins

Jot down **three** types of access control: systems or devices that enable organizations to control the entry of people to specified areas.

_____

_____

_____

_____

The simplest way to restrict entry is to put up some physical barrier, such as:

- locks and bolts
- perimeter fences and walls
- gates or barriers.

Other types of access control include:

> Remember that barring entry is a useless action if the thief is already inside!

- requiring everyone who has the right to enter an area to wear an identity badge;
- locking the area and issuing keys (or swipe-cards, or codes for electronic locks) to authorized people only;
- requiring all personnel who work in a certain area to wear an overall of a particular colour, so that visitors, or staff from another area, become very conspicuous.

If it isn't practical to restrict entry, there are still actions and attitudes to be taken which will reduce the opportunity to steal. You can:

- discourage loitering;
- be sure you know what, and how many, valuables you have, and keep them under close management: would-be thieves have less freedom to operate if they know that a theft will be spotted quickly;
- remove valuable goods from sight when they aren't being used;
- clamp or chain valuable equipment to benches or to the floor if practicable;
- keep areas well lit, perhaps even at night;
- insist that everything is accounted for, and not allow the issue of goods in bulk or as 'free issue'.

Limiting the opportunity for removal

Apart from reducing the opportunity to steal, the other way to make life difficult for thieves is to limit their opportunity to remove goods.

Anyone stealing anything from a place of work has to find a means of removing it from the premises. Methods for doing this may include:

- hiding a stolen article in clothing;
- walking out quite openly with it, acting as if he or she had a right do so;
- taking it out to a car in a car-park, perhaps during a break or lunch-hour;
- removing it using a company vehicle;
- posting it to a home address, simply by packaging up the article and taking it to the mail room!

Needless to say, this list is not exhaustive.

You need to be aware of these and other methods of smuggling goods out, and take appropriate actions to prevent them.

5.2 Some principles of good security

Let us now set out some principles which every organization should apply, in order to improve security.

- There should be a clear policy with regard to security

  The organization's policy must be made clear to all employees. A positive and open approach to security, including a policy for dealing with offences, will make most employees feel more secure, and will help to deter dishonest activities.

  The idea of security is to deter crime and reduce losses, not to catch thieves.

  In its **security policy** the organization should make the following points clear.

  - The organization recognizes that most of its employees are honest.

    Security measures should exist to protect the majority, not to try to catch them out. Employers won't succeed with security unless they believe they can trust most of their employees.

  - Security is a part of the job of every manager.

    It is not possible to 'hand over' security to a separate function, even when specialized security staff are employed. Security is a normal management function.

■ Just as much attention will be paid to the property of employees as that of the organization.

The property of employees must be protected as well as the property of the employer. Organizations should ensure that reasonable security is provided for employees' property while on company business.

■ There will be acceptable and lawful practices for dealing with disciplinary matters.

This is in any case an obligation on all employers. Suspected offenders must be fairly treated.

■ Security training will be provided for managers.

■ There will be a security manual which sets out approved procedures for dealing with all security matters.

■ Protection against loss of life and personal injury will be given bigger priority than protection of property.

■ **The level of security should be commensurate with the threat**

Every organization must have an acceptable level of security, regardless of its product. However, the security levels for more expensive goods should be higher than for less expensive ones.

Security costs money, and every organization must balance the cost of security with the threats and possible losses it is intended to combat.

■ **A good security measure should require more than one person to defeat it**

This is the principle of 'maximum complicity'. It means that the more people it takes to collaborate together to defeat a security measure, the better the measure is. To overcome a good security measure in the workplace, the collaboration of at least two people should be needed.

■ **A security system is only as strong as its weakest link**

It is said that 'fish always swim towards the hole in the net'. Too much attention on one aspect of security, and too little on another, can result in holes in security.

■ **Normal security should not get in the way of normal life**

The man who fits three locks to his front door, and leaves the back door open, should not be surprised to find that burglars have had no difficulty in getting in.

Security is not an end in itself. Security in the workplace should be designed to protect property, people, profits and jobs. It should not make life more difficult for the majority of people, and should not restrict normal activities.

■ **Employees need to be 'sold' the value of security**

Security is seldom a popular subject. While most managers realize the importance of security measures, and the reasons for them, others may not be so well-informed. Security can appear to be nothing more than an intrusion on everyday activities, or a management scheme to spy on employees.

61

Activity 29

5
mins

How might you go about 'selling ' the value of the organization's security measures to your team? Spend a few minutes thinking, and jot down your ideas on the subject.

_____

_____

_____

_____

_____

_____

If the organization has a written security policy covering the points we listed earlier, this should be explained to the team. You could also emphasize the facts that:

■ the protection of the organization's assets ultimately protects their own jobs and salaries;

■ it also is designed to help protect them and their possessions.

The workteam need to be told:

■ what security measures are in force;

■ why they are in force;

■ how they can help to implement and/or maintain the measures in their own areas.

There is a further important way you may win over doubters: by setting a personal example. You must be seen to:

■ be consistent and meticulous in following the security rules of the organization;

■ be firm but fair in all matters of discipline related to security;

■ never take company goods for your own use, however seemingly worthless they are;

■ co-operate fully with security staff, with other managers in security matters;

■ let the team know that you expect high standards of behaviour from them.

Activity 30

This Activity may provide the basis of appropriate evidence for your S/NVQ portfolio. If you are intending to take this course of action, it might be better to write your answers on separate sheets of paper.

Think about the security measures in your own job and workplace, and answer the following questions.

■ Do you know how much, if any, pilfering goes on? YES/NO

(If you don't know, then your methods of controlling and securing stock are probably inadequate.)

■ Have you had any problems with security over the past year or so? YES/NO

(If you have, then your security measures may be inadequate.)

■ How would you suggest security might be improved? Draft out a plan of action for improving security in your area, bearing in mind the principle that normal security should not get in the way of normal life. Your plan does not need to be longer than a page.

Self-assessment 3

I   Fill in the missing words in the diagram below:

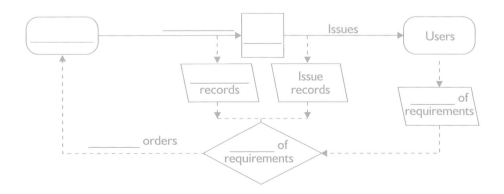

2 Match each name on the left with the correct comments, selected from the list on the right. More than one comment is associated with each name.

A Materials requirements planning (MRP)

B Electronic data interchange (EDI)

C Just-in-time (JIT)

D Automated guided vehicle (AGV)

a Enables buyers and suppliers to exchange a range of business documents including orders.

b Is concerned with the scheduling of activities and the management of stock.

c Is sometimes known as 'paperless trading'.

d May follow the path of wires laid beneath the floor.

e Produces schedules for activities and purchases as outputs.

f Produces forecast stock level as an output.

g Requires suppliers to make frequent deliveries, with very short lead-times.

h Enables the customer to minimize stocks held in a waiting area.

i Causes the customer's stock-holding costs to be passed to the supplier.

j Is typically employed in moving heavy or palleted goods.

3 Decide whether you agree or disagree with each of the following statements, which give advice on security. For those you do not agree with, give a short explanation of your reasons.

a 'If you turn a blind eye to petty pilfering, you are unlikely to have to worry about major theft.'

I agree ☐   I do not agree because:

_____

_____

_____

_____

b 'The best security measures are those that control or prevent entry to areas where valuable goods are.'

I agree ☐   I do not agree because:

_____

_____

_____

_____

c 'The idea of security is to catch thieves, not to deter crime and reduce losses.'

I agree ☐   I do not agree because:

_____

_____

_____

_____

d 'Every organization must balance the cost of security with the threats and possible losses it is intended to combat.'

I agree ☐   I do not agree because:

_____

_____

_____

_____

Answers to these questions can be found on pages 83–4.

6 Summary

- The functions of purchasing include:

  - finding new suppliers;
  - minimizing the cost of purchases;
  - arranging for goods to be delivered when and where they are needed;
  - maintaining good relations with suppliers and with other parts of the organization.

- The just-in-time system aims to minimize stock holding, and to demand supplies at the time and place they are needed, but not before they are needed. The system is only a practical proposition for large organizations with considerable 'buying power'.

- MRP (materials requirements planning) is:

  - mainly concerned with the scheduling of activities, and the management of stock;
  - is most useful where components and subassemblies are produced, for inclusion in the final product or service.

- Inputs to an MRP program are: the master schedule; a bill of requirements; the opening stock balances; a schedule of capacity. Outputs are: an activity schedule; a purchase schedule; a shortage list; forecast stock levels; forecast of spare or deficient capacity.

- MRPII (manufacturing resources planning mark II) goes much further than MRP, in that it is a method for planning all manufacturing resources.

- Four examples of technology in materials management are EDI (electronic data interchange); bar coding; CD ROMs; robots.

- Every organization is vulnerable to theft and other crime.

- The four conditions that must be present for an act of theft are: something to steal; a thief to do the stealing; the opportunity to steal; a means of removing the goods.

- An important principle of security is expressed by the phrase 'the need to know and the need to go'.

- Some important principles of security are:

  - There should be a clear policy with regard to security.
  - The idea of security is to deter crime and reduce losses, not to catch thieves.
  - The level of security should be commensurate with the threat.
  - A good security measure should require more than one person to defeat it.
  - A security system is only as strong as its weakest link.
  - Normal security should not get in the way of normal life.
  - Employees need to be 'sold' the value of security.
  - Managers should set an example by being seen to be scrupulously honest.

Performance checks

Jot down the answers to the following questions on *Controlling Physical Resources*.

Question 1   We listed nine types of resource. Name **five** of these.

_____

_____

_____

_____

_____

Question 2   Why might it be dangerous to treat people as just another resource?

_____

_____

_____

Question 3   What would you say to someone who wanted some good general advice on getting the best from equipment?

_____

_____

_____

Question 4   Explain the differences between raw materials, components and consumables.

_____

_____

_____

Question 5   Explain briefly what is meant by the statement: 'having stocks too high is bad news; having stocks too low may be worse news'.

_____

_____

_____

Question 6   What is meant by 'shrinkage'?

Question 7   Write down the book stock formula.

Question 8   What is the purpose of ABC analysis?

Question 9   Which **two** main types of transaction take place as a result of goods being received?

Question 10   What is the meaning of 'minimum stock'?

Question 11   'There are no real advantages for an organization in having a person or group that specializes in purchasing.' Briefly explain the reasons why you do, or do not, agree with this statement.

Question 12   Name **one** advantage, and **one** disadvantage, of the just-in-time system, from the point of view of the organization being supplied.

Question 13   List **one** input, and **two** outputs, of an MRP program.

68

Question 14   What are the **four** conditions that must be present if an act of theft or pilfering is to occur?

Question 15   What is meant by the phrase; 'a need to know and a need to go'?

Answers to these questions can be found on pages 84–5.

2 Workbook assessment

60 mins

Read the following case incident and then deal with the questions that follow, writing your answers on a separate sheet of paper.

■   AC Electrics is an independent company that, in its one plant, produces about 150 different consumer products. In many cases the difference between the products is only slight and the result of some modification. For example, they produce twelve models of vacuum cleaner.

The consumer market is extremely competitive and so it is essential, if it is to survive, for the firm to adopt a market-oriented policy. This is even more important for AC Electrics as they are one of the smaller firms in this business. To this end AC Electrics sell directly to wholesalers and large retailers throughout the country. These customers expect a high level of service and often require very fast deliveries. In order to meet these demands, AC Electrics established a number of regional warehouses, where stocks of all the products are held.

Three departments have responsibility for the control of stock:

■   The marketing department is responsible for the control of all finished goods both in the warehouses and at the plant. Through their direct contacts with existing and prospective customers and their market-research activities, they claim to be able to forecast the stock levels required for each product in each warehouse.
■   The production department is responsible for the control of stock required for production and also for work-in-progress. Production requirements consist mainly of bought-in components, together with a few raw materials such as packaging. The department's principal concern is to meet promptly the requirements of the marketing department to supply the regional warehouses. In order to meet this aim, production plans often have to be changed at relatively short notice.

69

■ The other department which has responsibility for stocks within AC Electrics is the purchasing department; this is concerned with maintenance stocks and works and office supplies. It does the buying for the production department. The purchasing department is not entirely happy with the short-term planning of the production department and its effect on purchasing costs. Generally, they believe that the organization is paying too much for components and materials, and that costs could be reduced if they could place orders in larger quantities.

1 Identify the likely costs associated with the above method of holding stocks.

2 Suggest **two** ways in which some of these costs might be reduced.

3 What advantages would AC Electrics gain by adopting a system of materials management such as MRP?

4 Do you think that stock-holding costs could be wholly or partly passed along to AC Electrics' suppliers? Explain your answer.

Portfolio of evidence B1.2

3 Work-based assignment

60 mins

The time guide for this assignment gives you an approximate idea of how long it is likely to take you to write up your findings. You will find you need to spend some additional time gathering information, perhaps talking to colleagues and thinking about the assignment.

Your written response to this assignment should form useful evidence for your S/NVQ portfolio. The assignment is designed to help you to demonstrate your personal competence in:

■ the ability to analyse and conceptualize, by showing that you can think clearly and objectively about the past, and to apply your thinking to present and future plans;
■ teambuilding skills;
■ the ability to focus on results;
■ the ability to think and take decisions.

What you have to do

Your aim is to put forward a concrete proposal designed to reduce your organization's costs related to the management of materials.

You may choose any aspect of the subject that we have discussed in this workbook. Then you will probably need to spend some time investigating and analysing the way things are done at present, and then identify an area where savings might be made. For example, you could examine the costs of shrinkage in the stores, or perhaps suggest that purchasing is carried out by a specialist, rather than by individual managers. Alternatively, you might look at documentation procedures.

If you aren't sure where to start, you might like to discuss possibilities with your tutor or your manager. If you want to look at an area outside your own sphere of control, no doubt you will have to seek permission from the relevant person first.

Write your work in the form of a short report, addressed to your manager.

Reflect and review

Now that you have completed your work on *Controlling Physical Resources*, let us review our workbook objectives.

This was our first objective:

■ When you have completed this workbook you will be better able to contribute to the management and control of resources in your organization.

We have looked, if only briefly in some cases, at a number of resources, and have highlighted a number of associated problems. As a manager, one of your principal functions is to organize and control resources effectively and efficiently.

Although we didn't devote much space to the management of people in this workbook, a couple of very important points were noted: the difficulties of developing people to their full potential; and the dangers of regarding employees as inanimate objects, to be handled without respect for their dignity as human beings.

Equipment, land, buildings, and materials, all require careful management, and, in the case of the first three, we identified a few ways in which they might be usefully dealt with.

Our main concern, however, has been with materials, and we have considered many aspects of the management of this resource.

You might like to think about the answers to the following questions.

■ How could you increase your skills in the management of people?

_____

_____

_____

■ How could you set about finding out more about the management of some of the other resources mentioned: equipment, time, energy, finance, land, buildings, information?

_____

_____

_____

73

- What will be your first step in contributing further to the control of resources in your organization?

_____

_____

_____

The second objective was:

- When you have completed this workbook you will be better able to explain the principles, and some ways of solving the problems, of stores and stock control.

The purpose of a store is as a buffer between the supplier and the user: between supply and demand. Holding stock, as we discussed, does not come cheap. In any small or medium-sized organization, however, it is an almost inescapable function. For large corporations, the costs and problems may be pushed onto the suppliers, using JIT.

Technology may help, and the increasing use of computers and other electronic devices, certainly enables organizations to reduce shrinkage and over-stocking. Useful techniques include those of ABC analysis, better documentation, and stock rotation. Everyday efficiency by teams and team leaders can do wonders for cost control.

- Which of the stock control techniques described in the workbook might be appropriate for your organization? How might you investigate it further?

_____

_____

_____

- Write down **one** problem in stores or stock control that you know about. How could you set about solving it?

_____

_____

_____

The third objective was:

- When you have completed this workbook you will be better able to increase your skills in various aspects of materials management.

Materials management entails much more than stores and stock control, and effective organizations take a broad-based view of the subject. Purchasing is one area: how can materials be obtained at minimum cost? In the production of goods and services, how can plans be made so that all operations run more efficiently? Would increased automation be an answer?

74

You may not be in a position to make large-scale plans for your organization, but you can try to improve the way things are run in your own work area, and you can take steps to increase your own knowledge and skills.

■ What specific aspects of materials management should you study further? How will you go about doing this?

_____

_____

_____

The final objective was:

■ When you have completed this workbook you will be better able to keep your resources more secure.

Security is a much-misunderstood aspect of management, and yet nearly all managers have responsibilities for seeing that materials and equipment are kept secure.

We covered a number of important principles, including:

■ the importance of a clear policy with regard to security, both within the organization as a whole, and in local work areas;
■ keeping the level of security commensurate with the threat;
■ the facts that a good security measure should require more than one person to defeat it, and that a security system is only as strong as its weakest link;
■ the necessity to recognize that normal security should not get in the way of normal life;
■ the need to 'sell' employees the value of security;
■ the importance of managers setting an example by being scrupulously honest.

■ Is there a need to make your work area more secure? If so, what are the first steps you will take to achieve this? (You may have answered this question in Activity 30.)

_____

_____

_____

2 Action plan

Use this plan to further develop for yourself a course of action you want to take. Make a note in the left-hand column of the issues or problems you want to tackle, and then decide what you intend to do, and make a note in Column 2.

The resources you need might include time, materials, information or money. You may need to negotiate for some of them, but they could be something easily acquired, like half an hour of somebody's time, or a chapter of a book. Put whatever you need in Column 3. No plan means anything without a timescale, so put a realistic target completion date in Column 4.

Finally, describe the outcome you want to achieve as a result of this plan, whether it is for your own benefit or advancement, or a more efficient way of doing things.

Desired outcomes					Actual outcomes
1 Issues	2 Action	3 Resources	4 Target completion		

3 Extensions

Extension 1

Book   *Storage and Supply of Materials*
Author   David Jessop and Alex Morrison
Edition   6th edition, 1994
Publisher Pitman

Jointly published with the Chartered Institute of Purchasing and Supply, this book 'seems to be firmly established as the standard book for practitioners and students . . . The contents have generally been brought up to date, with greater emphasis on health and safety and to relevant EC directives . . .' It is not difficult to read, and would be very useful to have on hand as a reference book, and something to dip into when you have time.

Extension 2

Standard   *BS5729: Guide to stock control*
Publisher British Standards Institute

BS5729 provides a useful summary of the fundamentals of stock control and storekeeping. Its five parts are:

- BS5729: Part 1: 1982. Introduction to management of stock control.

  Introduces the concepts and objectives of stock control as part of management strategy; outlines methods of setting target stock levels and their achievement.

- BS5729: Part 2: 1981. Demand assessment.

  Outlines some basic forecasting procedures for stock control.

- BS5729: Part 3: 1983. Replenishment of stock.

  Discusses the determination of stock replenishment policy, involving such parameters as order quantities, reorder systems and stock levels, reorder intervals and safety stocks. Some details of the materials requirement planning systems are given, together with the related subject of master scheduling.

- BS5729: Part 4: 1981. Data processing.

  Guidance on the application of data processing for personnel concerned with stock control.

- BS5729: Part 5: 1980. Storekeeping.

  Six major functions of storekeeping are identified within which a number of key tasks are listed in tables. Comments are made against each of these as an aid to setting up a store for those who are concerned with storekeeping within an organization.

Extension 3

Book   *Purchasing and Supply Management*
Author   P. J. H. Baily
Edition   5th edition, 1987
Publisher Chapman & Hall

If you are involved in, or interested in, the purchasing aspects of resource management, this book is worth looking at.

Extension 4

Book   *Essentials of Production and Operations Management*
Author   Ray Wild
Edition   1995
Publisher Cassell

This book has several sections relevant to our subject, including: the layout of facilities and materials handling; automated storage and retrieval; technology and work; capacity management; JIT; MRP; supply chain management; purchasing; inventory management.

These extensions can be taken up via your NEBS Management Centre. They will either have them or will arrange that you have access to them. However, it may be more convenient to check out the materials with your personnel or training people at work – they may well give you access. There are other good reasons for approaching your own people; for example, they will become aware of your interest and you can involve them in your development.

4 Answers to self-assessment questions

Self-assessment 1 on page 17

1 Compare your ticks with the table below:

	Materials	Equipment	People	Buildings	Land	Information	Energy	Finance	Time
Land					✓		✓		
Capital	✓	✓		✓		✓		✓	
Labour			✓						✓

2 The complete list is as follows.

The management of resources involves:

1 **DECIDING** what you want to achieve;
2 making **PLANS** to achieve it;
3 **SPECIFYING** the necessary resources;
4 locating and **ACQUIRING** those resources;
5 **PREPARING** the resources;
6 **CONTROLLING** and organizing the resources to best effect.

3 The completed puzzle is as follows:

```
 1                2  3                               4
 P        A  C  Q  U  I  R  E                    S
 E              O                                E
 5                                              6
 O  R  G  A  N  I  Z  A  T  I  O  N     S        R
 P              S                        P        V
 L        7                 8                     I
 L        E  Q  U  I  P  M  E  N  T      E        C
 E              M              N          C        C
          9                    E       10         E
          J              A              E     T  I  M  E  S
          O              B              R          I  F        S
         11
          B  U  I  L  D  I  N  G  S              I
          E              L              Y          C        12
         13 14                                     A        P
          T  O  O  L  S                            A        L
             F                  15        16       T        A
             T              I  N  F  O  R  M  A  T  I  O  N
             E                  R        N         O        S
             N                  K        D         N
```

(Across) 2 ACQUIRE, 5 ORGANIZATION, 7 EQUIPMENT, 10 TIMES, 11 BUILDINGS, 13 TOOLS, 17 INFORMATION.
(Down) 1 PEOPLE, 3 COST..., 4 SERVICES, 6 SPECIFIC..., 9 JOB, 12 PLANS, 14 OFTEN..., 16 LAND...

Self-assessment 2 on page 44

1   The words and word pairs are:

   ABC ANALYSIS
   GOODS
   ISSUE
   LEAD TIME
   ORDER
   PILFERAGE
   RECEIVE
   ROTATION
   STOCK CONTROL
   STORES

The completed puzzle is:

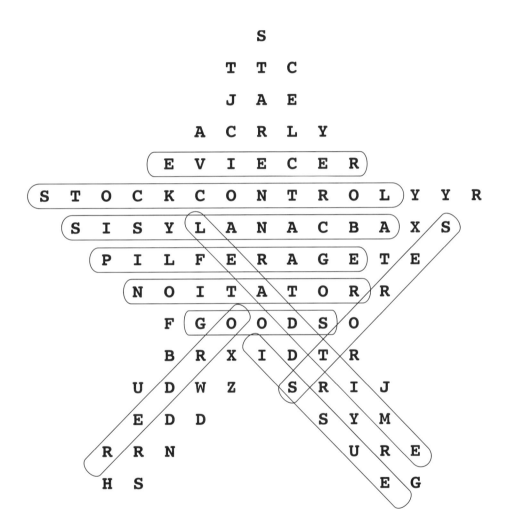

2   The only reason for holding stock is to have it ready for when it is needed. Because most goods take time to acquire (the lead-time), they may have to be ordered well in advance in order to bridge the gap between the supply and the demand.

3   The completed boxes are as shown:

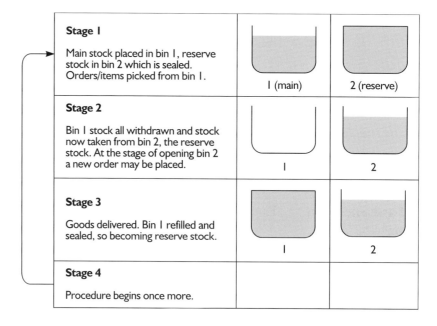

Stage 1		
Main stock placed in bin 1, reserve stock in bin 2 which is sealed. Orders/items picked from bin 1.	1 (main)	2 (reserve)
Stage 2		
Bin 1 stock all withdrawn and stock now taken from bin 2, the reserve stock. At the stage of opening bin 2 a new order may be placed.	1	2
Stage 3		
Goods delivered. Bin 1 refilled and sealed, so becoming reserve stock.	1	2
Stage 4		
Procedure begins once more.		

4   The usage values are:

Item	Unit cost (£)	Annual sales (£)	Usage value(£)
Vacuum cleaner	230	500	115,000
Microwave oven	340	750	255,000
Refrigerator	175	330	57,750
Installing kit	25	1000	25,000
Spares kit	45	120	5,400

5   ABC analysis is a means of categorizing items of stock on the basis of their usage value, where usage value is the cost of the item times the number issued or sold annually. ABC analysis is a modification of the Pareto principle, which shows that the bulk of value is likely to be held by a very small proportion of the total items. When the Pareto principle is applied to stock management, we usually adopt three categories, A, B and C, rather than the two categories of 80:20.

6 The completed sentences are as follows.

a Stock is a **BUFFER** between supply and **DEMAND**, or between the suppliers and the users.

b Organizations generally aim to keep the **MINIMUM** stocks in the minimum **SPACE** for the minimum time.

c Having stocks too **HIGH** is bad news; having stocks too **LOW** may be worse news.

d Opening stock + **PURCHASES** – issues = closing stock.

e In any store, about **20 PER CENT** of all the items held will account for about **80 PER CENT** of the usage value.

Self-assessment 3 on page 63

1 The completed diagram is:

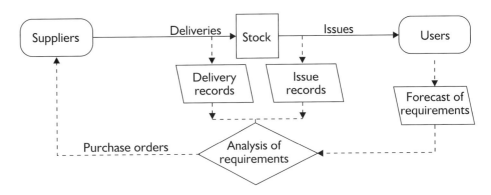

2   A Materials requirements planning (MRP)

    b Is concerned with the scheduling of activities and the management of stock.

    e Produces schedules for activities and purchases as outputs.

    f Produces forecast stock level as an output.

  B Electronic data interchange (EDI)

    a Enables buyers and suppliers to exchange a range of business documents including orders.

    c Is sometimes known as 'paperless trading'.

  C Just-in-time (JIT)

    g Requires suppliers to make frequent deliveries, with very short lead-times.

    h Enables the customer to minimize stocks held in a waiting area.

    i Causes the customer's stock-holding costs to be passed to the supplier.

  D Automated guided vehicle (AGV)

    d May follow the path of wires laid beneath the floor.

    j Is typically employed in moving heavy or palleted goods.

3 The least credible statements are:

a 'If you turn a blind eye to petty pilfering, you are unlikely to have to worry about major theft.'

Reason: There is no clear demarcation line between petty pilfering and theft, and even fairly honest people will tend to do what they think they can get away with. Far better advice is to make it clear that all pilfering is theft, and that it will not be tolerated.

b 'The best security measures are those that control or prevent entry to areas where valuable goods are.'

Reason: It is one kind of security measure, but may be quite inappropriate for normal work areas. In any case, having physical barriers won't help if the thief is already inside.

c 'The idea of security is to catch thieves, not to deter crime and reduce losses.'

Reason: This is exactly the opposite of good advice.

5 Answers to activities

Activity 13 on page 27

Perhaps you didn't have much trouble in answering as follows:

a 140 (opening stock) + 120 (purchases) – 160 (issues) = 100 (closing stock).
b Opening stock + purchases – sales = closing stock.
c 90 + 60 – 70 = 80.
d Opening stock + purchases – closing stock = issues (sales).

6 Answers to the quick quiz

Answer 1 You could have mentioned: people; equipment; land; buildings; finance; materials; information; energy; time.

Answer 2 The simple answer is that people do not respond well when they feel they are being treated like a piece of furniture or equipment. Managers who fall into this trap seldom succeed in their aims.

Answer 3 To get the optimum value from equipment, it is important for the people using it to have: a good understanding of what it is designed to do; training in how to use it; a proper system of maintenance; an appropriate system of security.

Answer 4 Raw materials are basic substances that are processed in order to manufacture products, such as wood and plastics. Components are parts, often having themselves been manufactured from raw materials, which go to make a larger assembly. Consumables are items that are used up in a work process, and do not necessarily form part of the final product.

Answer 5 If stocks are too high, money is tied up in goods that aren't being used. If stocks are too low, the organization's activities may be impeded, which may be potentially even more costly.

Answer 6 Shrinkage is losses and deterioration caused by: a decline in quality; goods becoming out of date; damage; pilferage.

Answer 7 The book stock formula is expressed as:

$$opening\ stock + purchases - issues = closing\ stock$$

Answer 8 ABC analysis is a method of determining the relative amount of attention that should be given to goods in stock. (You might also have mentioned that a usage value is calculated for each item, which is the purchase price times the number issued or sold; the highest usage value items receive the greatest amount of attention.)

Answer 9 There are two possible transactions involved in the receipt of goods: taking in new goods, just delivered by a supplier; and taking back old goods, which had been issued and which are now being returned for some reason.

Answer 10 The minimum stock is the lowest possible level you should hold to avoid any danger of running out.

Answer 11 There are real advantages to having purchasing specialists, including the facts that: it is a job requiring a good deal of expertise; it is important to build up good relationships with regular suppliers, and this takes time and effort; a specialist will be able to find suppliers for new items quickly; non-specialist managers won't waste time on purchasing tasks, which they have no training in.

Answer 12 Potential advantages include: lower inventory costs, lower handling costs, lower space costs, and increased productivity. Disadvantages are that it may be difficult to implement unless your organization has a lot of 'buying power', a great deal of planning is required, and if things ever go wrong, business may effectively come to a halt.

Answer 13 Inputs are: the master schedule (a forecast or actual demand for products or services); a bill of requirements (a list of all parts, materials, and services required for each product); the opening stock balances; a schedule of capacity (what the organization is capable of producing). Outputs are: an activity schedule (what has to be done); a purchase schedule (what has to be bought); a shortage list; forecast stock levels; forecast of spare or deficient capacity.

Answer 14 There must be: something to steal; a thief; the opportunity to steal; a means of removing the goods.

Answer 15 The phrase reminds us that: information that might be useful to lawbreakers should be restricted to those with a **need to know**; to maintain good security, it is best to restrict people to those areas where they **need to go**.

7 Certificate

Completion of this certificate by an authorized person shows that you have worked through all the parts of this workbook and satisfactorily completed the assessments. The certificate provides a record of what you have done that may be used for exemptions or as evidence of prior learning against other nationally certificated qualifications.

Pergamon Open Learning and NEBS Management are always keen to refine and improve their products. One of the key sources of information to help this process are people who have just used the product. If you have any information or views, good or bad, please pass these on.

NEBS
MANAGEMENT
DEVELOPMENT

SUPER SERIES

THIRD EDITION

Controlling Physical Resources

....

has satisfactorily completed this workbook

Name of signatory   ....

Position   ....

Signature   ....

Date   ....

Official stamp

SUPER SERIES

SUPER SERIES 3

0-7506-3362-X	Full Set of Workbooks, User Guide and Support Guide

A. Managing Activities

0-7506-3295-X	1. Planning and Controlling Work
0-7506-3296-8	2. Understanding Quality
0-7506-3297-6	3. Achieving Quality
0-7506-3298-4	4. Caring for the Customer
0-7506-3299-2	5. Marketing and Selling
0-7506-3300-X	6. Managing a Safe Environment
0-7506-3301-8	7. Managing Lawfully - Safety, Health and Environment
0-7506-37064	8. Preventing Accidents
0-7506-3302-6	9. Leading Change

B. Managing Resources

0-7506-3303-4	1. Controlling Physical Resources
0-7506-3304-2	2. Improving Efficiency
0-7506-3305-0	3. Understanding Finance
0-7506-3306-9	4. Working with Budgets
0-7506-3307-7	5. Controlling Costs
0-7506-3308-5	6. Making a Financial Case

C. Managing People

0-7506-3309-3	1. How Organisations Work
0-7506-3310-7	2. Managing with Authority
0-7506-3311-5	3. Leading Your Team
0-7506-3312-3	4. Delegating Effectively
0-7506-3313-1	5. Working in Teams
0-7506-3314-X	6. Motivating People
0-7506-3315-8	7. Securing the Right People
0-7506-3316-6	8. Appraising Performance
0-7506-3317-4	9. Planning Training and Development
0-75063318-2	10. Delivering Training
0-7506-3320-4	11. Managing Lawfully - People and Employment
0-7506-3321-2	12. Commitment to Equality
0-7506-3322-0	13. Becoming More Effective
0-7506-3323-9	14. Managing Tough Times
0-7506-3324-7	15. Managing Time

D. Managing Information

0-7506-3325-5	1. Collecting Information
0-7506-3326-3	2. Storing and Retrieving Information
0-7506-3327-1	3. Information in Management
0-7506-3328-X	4. Communication in Management
0-7506-3329-8	5. Listening and Speaking
0-7506-3330-1	6. Communicating in Groups
0-7506-3331-X	7. Writing Effectively
0-7506-3332-8	8. Project and Report Writing
0-7506-3333-6	9. Making and Taking Decisions
0-7506-3334-4	10. Solving Problems

SUPER SERIES 3 USER GUIDE + SUPPORT GUIDE

0-7506-37056	1. User Guide
0-7506-37048	2. Support Guide

SUPER SERIES 3 CASSETTE TITLES

0-7506-3707-2	1. Complete Cassette Pack
0-7506-3711-0	2. Reaching Decisions
0-7506-3712-9	3. Managing the Bottom Line
0-7506-3710-2	4. Customers Count
0-7506-3709-9	5. Being the Best
0-7506-3708-0	6. Working Together

To Order - phone us direct for prices and availability details
(please quote ISBNs when ordering)
College orders: 01865 314333 • Account holders: 01865 314301
Individual purchases: 01865 314627 (please have credit card details ready)